LIFE SPACE

John M Hunter

LIFE SPACE

Printed in Canada by Sure Print & Design

I dedicate this book

to all those who seek

to learn and grow

AND

To the victims of the

Yonge Street Massacre

That occurred on

April 23, 2018,

In Toronto, Canada

CONTENTS

Preface 7

Introduction 9

Part One

About Critical Intent 21

Part Two

Preparation and Training Ground for the Focused

Intent and Implementation of Critical Intent 31

Part Three

Critical Intent and Bull's-eye Vision Together 57

Part Four

My Story 77

Part Five

Why Critical Intent 87

Part Six

Sustaining Critical Intent 117

The Death of Charlie 123

LIFE Space 125

Conclusion 129

Contacting the Author 133

PREFACE

The recent vehicular homicide in Toronto's Yonge Street that claimed the lives of 10 innocent victims and injured 14, some critically, on April 23, 2018, was by itself horrific. What words of comfort can we give to the victims of this tragic event? The mourning, and memorial services held at the vicinity of where the van attack took place, was a demonstration of Toronto's citizens coming together in unity, voicing their sympathy and support for the affected victims and families, whose lives are forever changed.

Upon my own reflection of the whole event, and the unfolding of what has come about since the incident, gives rise to this book, "Life Space," as a way in which I can contribute, to the healing process and, offer a way forward for of all of us to become better persons within our own lives and thus positively effect the lives of others, who cross our path moment to moment. And hence I dedicate this book to all the victims of the Yonge Street massacre.

This book offers a way in which, you the reader, will come away with two valuable tools, which I have called, 1) Critical Intent, and 2) Bull's eye-vision, that will become a compass to navigate your way forward toward a better place, where you, your family, and surrounding community, will begin to expand and grow within yourself, and at the same time, will positively impact others who cross your path moment to moment. Critical Intent and Bull's eye-vision are a remarkable resource that will help you develop the laser-beam focus you need to be able to truly reach out to and care for the people you encounter in your daily life. My no-nonsense approach singles out the struggles we all face to overcome the negative aspects of life and realize our potential as victorious, influential people. This real and powerful method teaches you how to nurture a continuous intention to really see people, touch hearts and minds for the better, and develop the vision you need to best meet the needs of others. Both challenging and encouraging, this exceptional resource will open up your eyes to a new and hope-filled way of living and looking at life.

INTRODUCTION

MY DISCOVERY OF CRITICAL INTENT

LET ME TELL you my story concerning the discovery and journey of Critical Intent.

This is what I call my dog experience which, took place one day in August 2013 while I was walking my dog, Charlie (Half beagle, half hound) loves to be out walking, sniffing with his nose to the ground, as is his tendency, for the aromatic delights that nature has to offer. It's interesting to see him come across the scent of a rabbit and to witness the instinctual reaction that such a dog produces.; I hold on to the leash for starters.

Our neighborhood in Scarborough (now considered Toronto, Ontario, since amalgamation) is nothing special, your average community neighborhood in Toronto, that hosts varying cultural and ethnic mixes, indicative of Toronto's cosmopolitan-defining character. There lives in this vast mix of such diversity those who, for whatever reason, are not a dog's best friend. In coming upon other's walking space with Charlie, I found a distasteful disgust that ignited the two of us, so that we walked away from each other, with the one who freely showed their displeasure of my intrusion into their space with my dog, will probably not even consider their rudeness to a neighbor, and simply carry on in their world of indifference and contempt regarding fellow neighbors, while I, boil with anger.

Through the many years, have I had such encounters with those who choose to ignore and bypass the opportunity to exchange a friendly gesture of neighborly greeting. On this day in August 2013, when I encountered yet again another look of contempt. I, as expected, experienced the same bubbling up of anger. But this time I stopped and challenged, not the person whom I came across-that person was gone and out of the picture-but solely challenged my own condition. Why, I asked myself, react in anger at such encounters? I had allowed myself to be in the grip of anger by someone else who, was simply calmly walking along, oblivious to my state of anger. I silently screamed and penetrated the depths of the universe in seeking an answer to open myself beyond the confines of a lesser self.

Then from out the blue came the answer.

Because you do not care enough about people!!!

That's it, I said to myself. It's true; I do not care enough about people. The answer was a gift of insight, grabbing and catapulting me to an illuminated realization of the truth and answer to my question. By generating a focused intent of caring for the person before me, moment to moment, would enable my higher self to squash- put at bay my lesser self, allowing me to move forward to a bright path impacting not only myself, but also, whomever crosses my path moment to moment.

From then on, I said to myself, whomever crosses my path will generate from me the focused intent of caring for that person with my entire being. I determined to train my mind to focus and seek out the aspect of caring for others. I was riding the laser beam of a focused intent of caring for the person before me. Such touching will inevitably cast the imprint of humanity's long forgotten caring, that marks the highest honor of our place to be, moment to moment, in the engagement of our jeweled resources to direct our capacity as a human being to care for the person before us, on our stage of play, here on earth.

I was on cloud nine, for I felt that I had now found a path of direction, that I could now confidently lead. Everything that had gone before me in terms of my experiences and learning could now have value in integrating the bits and pieces of my life into a life of purpose and direction.

I then proceeded to continue walking, maintaining the focused determination to unleash a laser beam of focused intent of caring to the first person whom I would inevitably encounter. But before that took place, suddenly my dog pulled me across the street. My dog, by the way, always stays on one side of the street while we do a complete circle of the street crescent. But for some reason, unexpectedly at that moment, I was then being led somewhere. Soon, in a matter of about ten seconds, I found myself approaching a gentleman who was just standing in his driveway. Unavoidably, Charlie stopped, before the stranger. It did not take long for me to realize what was happening. This was an opening passage to a new dimension, to a new opening path for my life to move into. It was the realm of applying the focused intent of caring for whomever would cross my path moment to moment.

The situation then was obvious. I was meant to engage, fully, with this individual before me. Charlie sat patiently as I began to engage in conversation. Amicably and naturally, we exchanged common conversation. But this time there was something different going on between two people. There was no awkwardness of acceptance of who we were, instead, there was simply a warm embrace of natural cohesion between two individuals. It was that someone sincerely took the initiative in recognizing a fellow neighbor, talking and taking the time to go out of their way to make a difference in someone else's life. Nothing noteworthy came about from the content of the small talk, but within the small talk, lay an opening ground for life-to-life, heart-to-heart communication. between two individuals. My dog indicated that it was now time to go, and we parted our ways; my dog pulled me across the street where we were formerly walking, as if to say, mission completed.

This event was a very powerful demonstration of the immediate transforming power that takes place when we have a change of mind or, more specifically, when we decide to generate the magnitude of our life toward the focused intent of caring for another who crosses our path, moment to moment. A confirmation of mystical proportions had taken place, substantiating and reinforcing the answer to my question, of how I could break away from the cycle of a self-centered, reactionary anger, to an outside stimulus.

Soon after this dog experience, I sat down and wrote a poem to encapsulate the essence of Critical Intent:

Generating with my whole being

Gathering up the energies of my soul

In commanding the focus of my mind

My mind and heart infusing to the heart of another

The intent of my caring for what lays before me

Opens up and lays bare the battle before me

Like a laser beam of clarity

I perceive the darkness, the bastion of resistance

That cannot hide from the shining light of a caring heart.

My heart meshes into the hearts of others

The thawing, the shock, the movement toward, a better place

A pause of direction, a stillness in time

As what existed before is submerged for now

As a new emergence of an expanded heart takes place.

As we part, the seed of a caring intent has been planted.

May the water and nutrition that you so inherently hold

Begin to nurture and grow

So that you may glow

To become the person

Who everybody knows.

Each contact with a human being is so rare,

so precious, one should preserve it.

-ANAIS NIN

No one care until someone cares; be that one!

-KEN POIROT

Memories of our lives, of our works and

our deeds will continue in others.

-ROSA PARKS

I'm at peace with myself in knowing that within the context of living our interactions with others, that I'm able to present to you a valuable and powerful tool, called Critical Intent, enabling you to live your life, where both yourself and others, will come to begin a movement toward an expanded and better life. At once, at peace within the context of our living interactions with others, do we find the tool of caring that so decisively mounts a tool-of deliverance into the hearts of others. The tool of Critical Intent, the focused intent in caring for others comes about when we come face to face with whomever happens to cross our path moment to moment.

Not to confuse the caring for others, as a form of charity, such as providing money, food, clothing and housing etc., all valuable acts of necessity and kindness, but rather in living each moment with the powerful and transformative mindset and focus that will enable you to penetrate to the core and depths of another person's heart who crosses your path.

Life is a constant battle requiring the constant engagement of our jeweled resources to shatter and redirect the constant movement of our inherent darkness and negativity, toward the light and positivity that comes about when we direct our focused intent to care for the person before us at any moment. In so doing, we become the master to slay the dark beast of our discomfort and weakness that comes about all too often, when we engage ourselves with others.

This book will teach you, step by step, the required process and training needed to practice Critical Intent. In the process, you will gain the added benefit of learning a technique that I developed called Bull's-eye vision, which being both essential in practicing Critical Intent, and for allowing you to penetrate with an x-ray type of perception/vision to unmask the façade that others hold as their appearance.

You hold the key to your great potential waiting to be unleashed into the hearts of others. The jewels of wisdom, confidence, perception, fulfillment, conviction, and compassion to name a few, all come about when you begin the practice of Critical Intent. Be patient and open minded in considering your new, found entry into the possible tool of Critical Intent. My no nonsense, no holes barred approach addresses what needs to be said and done, in the world in which we live. Once you become equipped with a new resource of engagement toward others, then others will be your new vehicle upon which you share the welling up of your great potential from within your life.

I invite you to join me, in reaching out to others, who are waiting and in need of your appearance, at this critical time in which we now live. This book will teach you the essential tool of Critical Intent, enabling you, at once, to break open the powerful sun residing in your heart toward an unknown multitude of others, waiting for your arrival.

Why Critical Intent

This book lays bare the critical necessity for us as humans to have a consideration for the importance of having a focused intent of caring for those who cross our path moment to moment in our daily life. Why Critical Intent, helps to clarify why the focused intent of caring for others is critical for the well being of our individual lives in all aspects of our life. Well being in the context of our life, now, is not to be glossed over as a catch for all cliché-well being, but as a critical necessity that we attempt, at least, partially to have a mindset conducive to the focused parameters involving other's well being-that in accordance with the workings of life, will in return, benefit the well being of our own life. Taking from the abstracted idea of the focused intent in caring for others, to the concrete application-scientific if you will, is the purpose and construction of this book, providing a holistic structure from which the magnitude of your life can flourish.

JUST IMAGINE

What if you were to be given a tool that would allow you to be the person that you want to be? Yes, you can be that person. Just imagine that you are:

At peace with yourself

Having harmony in your relationships

Living with confidence, wisdom, courage, and caring

Being an outstanding, attractive light to others

Living to your full potential

Being a leader to others

Living an abundant life

There's more to this list. Sit down and challenge me about the truth of such boldness. Prepare yourself to read, explore, and feel the power of who you really are. Take a step forward into my world of discovery. Live my life that I share with you. Consider my experience as one with your own life experience. Ignite the dormancy in your life, stand tall, take a stand, and move forward in the direction of your grand partaking. Ignite the feelings of your discontent to burn forth a new path, a new direction, to liberate you in your momentum, away for the prison of your mind, to the full harmony of both body and mind, working together to liberate you from passivity and stagnation. The earthquake of your awakening, will shake and rattle the dusty relics of your domain.

The tool of Critical Intent awaits your taking up the weapon to battle the darkness that pervades your life and, that of others. Your entry into the midst of those around you will also shake, rattle, and vibrate to the tune of your newfound harmonic domain. To the point, directly to the core, will I take you. Fast and furious, gradual and accommodating, clear and comprehensible is what lies bare before you.

Somewhere, something incredible is waiting to be

Known

-CARL SAGAN

PART ONE

ABOUT CRITICAL INTENT

Memories of our lives, of our works and
our deeds will continue in others.
-ROSA PARKS

The purpose of learning about Critical Intent is to enable one to discover the value of having the focused intent in caring for others, and in learning how to apply that focused intent in one's daily life.

The message of caring is simple, but can we maintain throughout our daily life a continuous intent of caring for another human being? What does it take for us to freely live our life with such an honorable virtue as caring for another person who crosses our path? Part of the challenge is in addressing the inner workings of our own life that limit and prevent us from achieving such a noble virtue as caring for another person. Being mindful of our negative/dark tendencies, places us in a position of clarity, steering us in a better direction.

Just being nice and easy to get along with, although good qualities, will not cut it when it comes to living in today's world. We need to be strong and confident in our relationships and dealings with others. Living with the ongoing intent of caring for others enables us to successfully manage the intricate complexities and demands that impinge upon us throughout our everyday life, because the aspects of wisdom, confidence, and perception become our sword of battle to cut through the inevitable entanglements that we encounter day to day.

By becoming good examples, others are touched by our presence, and the positive change awakes to others, a surge of beauty, admired and defined.

Critical Intent is an ongoing intent to care for the person appearing before one in the present moment. The intent of caring for another, manifests from within us, a powerful life force, that goes beyond self, to touch and embrace the person before us.

As we go about radiating our intent of caring for others, we at the same time manifest from within our life many valuable qualities, such as wisdom, compassion, courage, and confidence. Each moment we become the masters of our minds. Our minds are directed to keep on track in living each moment, the focused intent of caring for others who cross our path; critical because, the absence of such, allows our unenlightened self, to rein over our every moment. Our intent is critical for our own development and growth in becoming a person who emanates the qualities of a caring person. And, by becoming a caring person, the outward spreading of touching others, will in turn create a positive change in society.

Walking with a friend in the dark is better

than walking alone in the light.

-HELEN KELLER

BEING HUMAN AND A HERO TO OTHERS

The purpose of human life is to serve, and to show

Compassion and the will to help others.

-ALBERT SCHWEITZER

WHAT DOES IT MEAN TO BE HUMAN?

Well, of course, you are human, but are you living your life to the best that you can be as a human? What qualities do I need to be worthy of being called truly human, and how does being human relate to Critical Intent?

In a nutshell, a person who has the focused intent of caring for others, and whose life capacity expands beyond their self-centered disposition-thus expanding their life space in reaching out to others, regardless of who they are, is the mark of being truly human, and is the mark of a person practicing Critical Intent.

Being truly human does not mean anything special or out of the ordinary. But, rather, by our own volition to penetrate through the darkness that impedes our focused intent of caring for the individual before us, do we then exhibit the power that comes about from within and without. A transformation takes place not only from within ourselves, as we exert our full energized focus to the person before us, but it also occurs for the person appearing before us, who cannot help but be touched in some way. You have made a casual input, and the effects of such will manifest positively from without, in the sense, that, both the person before you and that person's surrounding environment will in some way be moved, or changed, from darkness toward goodness and light.

Let's take for example, the characters Superman, Superwoman, Batman, Bat woman, Spider-Man, Wonder Woman, etc. What all these characters have in common is their mission to unite humanity in the quest for justice, protection, peace, and harmony in the lives of ordinary citizens. We can all unite behind such principled values of goodness toward our fellow citizens.

Such superheroes carry out as their mandate the coming to the aid of those in need. This is not to be dictated by an automatic handout of material assistance to the person in need. Being such a superhero is not to be confused with charity work in terms of providing, for example, food, shelter, money, clothing, etc. Rather, a superhero appears before a chance encounter, in a moment in time, with whomever crosses the superhero's path, offering for example, words of encouragement and comfort to one in despair, or providing a listening ear of acknowledgement and understanding, and sometimes advice. There is no limit to the range of help that an individual can offer to someone in need. The focused intent of caring for another, will in turn strengthen your own aspects of wisdom, compassion, and courage, which will in turn, well up from within, providing an output of action toward the individual in need, and consequently a positive thread has been created that will impact favorably both the superhero (that is you) and the person's life that you have just touched.

Amongst the qualities a hero should have, I would Include determination, loyalty, courage, perseverance, Patience, focus, intrepidity, and selflessness.
-RICKY MARTIN

The only thing necessary for the triumph of evil is for Good men to do nothing.
-EDMUND BURKE

Life shrinks or expands in proportion to one's courage
-ANAIS NIN

CRITICAL INTENT, NOT CHARITY WORK

CRYING IN NEED of material assistance can be heard throughout societies. Charity functions to alleviate this need for assistance. The noble workers who put their heart and soul into providing for those in need is commendable. However, let me point out that the function and role of Critical Intent is not charity in the classical sense. To mix the role of Critical Intent with charity is to miss the point of Critical Intent. Critical Intent does not exclude charity work entirely. For example, an individual who exercises the focused intent of caring for the person at hand may decide to partake in some form of material assistance, be it food, money, housing, etc. But this type of assistance is solely an individual's choice. As a practitioner of Critical Intent, one is not mandated by any directive, or expectation, to engage in charity work. Critical Intent engages one to break the ice of a suffering heart, that has closed itself off, due to a sinister progression of alienation, insincerity, greed, and self-centeredness, that is like a plague, ripping out the heart of our humanity.

The focused intent of caring for the person before you, acts as the critical antidote to stir and ignite the light of goodness, innocence, trust, and hope, to name a few, that all reside in each of us. It is up to individuals to manifest and demonstrate through their behavior, the beginning place that starts the creation toward individuals sharing and becoming the magnificent beings that they are. The power of even one caring person can, by touching others, transmit a causal input, that will begin the building toward a society of caring. It starts with each one of us, bursting out upon the stage of our humanity to bring forth our shinning light to penetrate through the iced darkness currently pervading our society these days.

PART TWO

PREPERATION AND TRAINING GROUND FOR THE FOCUSED INTENT AND IMPLEMENTATION OF CRITICAL INTENT

BULL'S-EYE VISION

The new limitations are the human ones of perception

-MILTON BABBITT

Figurative style:

Shout, by Edvard Munch,1893.

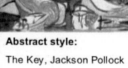

Abstract style:

The Key, Jackson Pollock

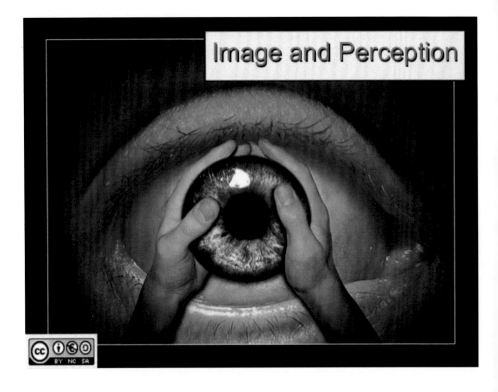

BULL'S-EYE VISION (BEV FOR SHORT) is a name that I came to use. By its two words, "Bull's-eye" and "vision," implies something related to perception. Learning how to focus on a specific intent, image, and thought is crucial to Critical Intent. It is important that your focus be as laser beam directed as possible. BEV will give you the focus needed to penetrate outward beyond your own deluded tainted vision. Perceiving the true reality of one's environment and the person at hand, allows one the upper hand in harmonizing and connecting with the person at hand who crosses their path moment to moment. The technique of Bev serves as a perceptual tool that enables one to have what you might call x-ray vision into the depths of a person's manifesting condition in the present moment. A person's emotional state, frame of mind, and exhibited behavior, can all be perceived within a matter of seconds, when one's focus is directed and concentrated sufficiently toward the person in question. When you know what to look for in a person's life, and have the clear focus of such, then lo and behold, a new dimension of perception, appears before your eyes. Learning how to focus effectively, requires a training ground of preparation for the eventual use of Critical Intent-which this book will teach to you. A well-trained body, for example, would be required if one were attempting to scale a mountain. In like manner, a well-trained ability to focus impartially, seeking the true reality of a manifesting condition before one's eyes, is necessary for one to be effective in utilizing the tool of Critical Intent in one's life.

The voyage of discovery is not in seeking new landscapes

But in having new eyes.

-MARCEL PROUST

A PERCEPTUAL TOOL

BEV is a pinpointing tool that measures and perceives instantly, human attributes being manifested by an individual in the present moment. In terms of BEV'S boundaries and range of perception, it is important to point out that even though one's targeted attribute can be detected in the moment, we cannot say for example that even though one's attribute of anger is manifesting, that the person is an angry person by nature. All of us as humans have the inherent potential to display a wide range of anger, depending on the situation. At the same time, we all inherently possess the quality of calmness and peacefulness. However, if we are pressed to assess weather or not the person evaluated is angry, by nature, then we would need to have a broader interaction with the person in question. We could view one human attribute like a pendulum. Let's say that a pendulum had the ability to reflect and measure an attribute residing in an individual at any given time. Based on some type of measuring device, we might find that the pendulum tends to rest at a certain point, most of the time. We then might be able to say that the person in question-for example, in the case of anger-has an angry character or disposition. But that analysis is not absolute or definitive regarding any person in question. That's because as humans, we all have the potential to change from within whatever negative or dark aspects of our life that we are presently living. Such a conquest of positive change within us, is the challenge that societies, cultures, religions a and philosophies have been attempting to temper since civilizations first emerged. Armed with the valuable tool of BEV, we can conquer the analysis of perception, that has alluded and frustrated us all too often.

TAKING CHARGE OF OUR PERCEPTION

There are things known and there are things unknown,

And in between are the doors of perception

-ALDOUS HUXLEY

BEV opens the doors to a new dimension of perception, enabling others to be seen from a different perspective. In using BEV, we do not become fixed, attached, or bonded to the appearance of the person before us. We break away form being passively unfocused and reactionary to whomever we encounter. By taking charge in directing our perception from within, we at the same time are thus able to accurately place our focus and perception onto whomever we encounter. We direct and command the focused image to place itself on a spot, where, the placement of the image, together with our directed focus, will reveal to us, the depths of the manifesting attribute to the Nth degree. The placement spot is the key to unleash the visual perception that will take place, (to be addressed later in the book.) The focussed image is specific and directed, thus cutting out the extraneous, and pinpointing the relevant. Nothing can stop the focused image from unmasking the unseen; the cover of our hiding crumbles and lays bare to the light of our focused intent. And so, by taking the strong initiative in directing and focusing our perception, we are no longer at the mercy of a distorted and unreliable perception of others.

What I had to learn was, that I'm responsible for my

perception of things.

-CHRIS ROBINSON

BENEFITS OF LEARNING BEV.

HOW BEV WILL HELP US

BEV acts as a tool that we can use when needed. The tool of BEV grants one the ability to see very clearly through false entanglements that usually define our perceptual limitations. False entanglement is a state in which we falsely read and interpret someone, and consequently our actions and decisions stemming from such a deluded perception entangle us even further into a web of further restricted movement rather than to a better place in our life.

One reason so few of us achieve what we truly want is

That we never direct our focus; we never concentrate our

power. Most people dabble their way through life, never

deciding to master anything in particular.

-TONY ROBBINS

PERCEPTUAL IMPEDIMENT

All of us show bias when it comes to what information

we take in. We typically focus on anything that agrees

with the outcome we want.

-NOREENA HERTZ

In this treacherous world

Nothing is the truth nor a lie.

Everything depends on the color

Of the crystal through which one sees it.

-PEDRO CALDERON DE LA BARCA

GENERALLY SPEAKING, OUR view of others is influenced by our own personal experiences, the exposure of our upbringing, our acquired learning, and the generally accepted views of the world that we have come to internalize. As such, true perceptual objectivity of others is compromised. Our perception tends to be tainted and biased, thus rendering true objectivity unlikely to be achieved; as such, our perception of others can be likened to being in a dense forest where our focus, for example, is on the thickness of the forest before us. In other words, our focus is drawn to our bias, to our emotional experiences of the past where both bias and emotion operate to create the dense forest that consumes our perception. Our perceptual senses are swamped and obliterated by the impinging impact of our immediate environment. We fail to locate a clear path or opening to direct our focus. Although unique individual attributes are being displayed to our sense of sight, our clarity of what we see is colored by an immovable dense forest, figuratively speaking. Our focus is scattered, weak, non-penetrable, and not specifically directed. We do not see beyond the immediate appearance impinging upon our visual senses. Again, we become swallowed up, consumed, stunned, and frozen by the stimulus of another's appearance, and for that reason we become drawn to any number of deluded conclusions we have about the person before us; so, we see the person before us, but, in a sense, at the same time, do not really see the true nature being exhibited before our eyes. In addition to our own bias, other's masquerade, shadows the clarity of our perception. In our perception, we have no positional basis in which to operate. There is no organization to our perception, no proactiveness, only a passive, reactive, and lazy fall of compliance to join others in their folly of missing the mark; the mark that comes about when we generate a seeking and directed focused intent, to see the truth manifesting in the person right before our eyes, moment to moment.

If the doors of perception were cleansed everything

Would appear to man as it is, Infinite. For man has

Closed himself up, till he sees all things thro' narrow

Chinks of his cavern.

-WILLIAM BLAKE

WHY DOES BEV WORK

BEV works because of our capability in producing a clear and penetrating focus on a specific target. The clarity of our image, coupled with our desire to seek the objective truth about a human attribute residing in a person, combine to allow an open reading, so transparent, that it is as if, we are seeing through the mask of one's outer appearance, into some sort of intuitive realm of clarity and certainty, that even myself, find it hard to describe in words. Bev works because, we as humans, when trained with the proper technique, practice, desire and effort, can transcend, as in the case of BEV, into an unknown point of entry that unravels before us, hidden aspects of the human condition.

-Look at everything always as though you were seeing it

either for the first or last time, then your time on earth

Will be filled with glory.

-BETTY SMITH, A TREE GROWS IN BROOKLYN

ASPECTS OF THE MIND

Breaking away from the outside and operating from the inside

When operating in the mode of BEV, we must seriously consider the following requirements of disengagement:

1) Disengage from what is happening on the outside.
2) Disengage from any emotional bonding to others.
3) We must be in control of our wandering mind.
4) Disengage all thoughts, and fiercely generate a clear and focused image.

It is one of the commonest of mistakes to consider that

The limit of our power of perception is also the limit of

All there is to perceive.

-C. W. LEADBEATER

OK---------LET'S START

Applying BEV

CLEARING, SETTLING AND
QUIETING THE MIND

You are now in the driver's seat. You are directing the course of where you want to go in your visual exploration. You steer your vision into the realms, into the secret hiding places-between the lines, so to speak-so that you can find the nature of people's attributes. Your x-ray vision instantly penetrates through the myriad of outer appearances that come before you. You must stop, take deep breaths, breathe slowly, and relax your whole being. Clear your mind of all thoughts. The only thought that you should have, is your determination to seek the truth- your determination to penetrate deep into the realm where one's attributes will be revealed and seen naked to bare. Relax and build up your determination. All other thoughts should be out of your mind as you begin to rev up the engine of your focus. Pour energy and power into your focus. There is silence in your mind; your hands are warm and relaxed right to the fingertips. Your blood is circulating well throughout your body. You are poised to shoot out, to leap out like a tiger in wait to catch its prey. Silence falls, and stillness permeates your being as you prepare to begin BEV.

Only in quiet waters things mirror themselves

Undistorted. Only in a quiet mind is adequate

Perception of the world.

-HANS MARGOLIS

MAINTAINING AND HOLDING

ONTO AN IMAGE

Hold fast to an image, and let it be the only image in your mind. I have a list of ten major categories/attributes that I personally have worked with, but of course you can add or choose any attribute that you choose. I suggest that you try the first attribute that I list, *"humanity."* I will give you a guide to help you create a clear image of what you can visualize as being humanity.

HUMANITY

Remember that you are asking the pertinent question silently to yourself regarding the person before you. You are not questioning your own humanity, but the humanity of the person in front of you.

What follows is a list of questions that I have used and found helpful when focusing and applying BEV to the aspect of humanity:

1) What is your concern and caring for others?

2) What is your awareness of the welfare of others?
3) Are you thinking of or considering the happiness of others?
4) Are you stepping outside of yourself and considering or contemplating the experience and condition of others?
5) Are you concerned about world events that affect the well-being of humanity?
6) Does your heart go out to other people?
7) Do you wish the best for humanity?
8) Is your life broad and open to embrace and comfort humanity?

Notice that the above listed questions, are very similar to each other. It is your choice to create the pertinent question that works for you. You only need to ask one question, that fits the kind of image that works for you. I have only rephrased the question into different possible wording. Every question that I have listed, refers to the aspect of humanity. But you can create your own question, that may very well be differently phrased than the above examples.

NOW let this chosen, created image of humanity be your vehicle of travel. Ride the waves and current of this image. This powerful image will lead you into the very depths of another's operating attribute of humanity. This image is your x-ray to go through all appearances. Keep this image in your mind's eye, and do not let it go. Disengage from any surrounding distractions. You are now in a place of absolute quietness, where time has stopped; only in a surreal way, are you totally meshed and united with the image that you have conjured in your mind's eye. Walk about and encounter different people, and at the same time do not abandon and get off the powerful vehicle of the selected image that you gave chosen.

We are enslaved by anything we do not consciously see.

We are freed by conscious perception.

-VERNON HOWARD

NOW FOR THE SECRET AND POWER OF BEV

TRANSFERING AN IMAGE

1)The image of humanity is now in your holding. Apply this image that you hold, shifting it directly onto the face, particularity to the eyes of the person whom you are evaluating. Later, as you become more adept, you will find that you can get an instant reading in focusing almost anywhere on the face.

2) Continually maintain the image as it permeates, surrounds, penetrates and meshes with the person's eye area. The interacting and meshing of the image will lock and fit onto their face.

3) You will see, and/or feel, how the image matches, meshes, or fits on their face. How does the image resonate with the likeness of what you see? Is the image of humanity at odds with, not matching or meshing, with the person before you? When the image is placed upon one's face, an instant readout takes place. How the image of humanity resonates or vibrates, will be your indicator of humanities place of existence in the moment, now, in the person before you.

4) In order to maintain the clarity of the image, it is sometimes necessary for you to repeat the question over in your mind more than once. For example, as you hold on to an image of humanity, you repeat the question: What is your humanity? What is your humanity? Unless you keep asking the question in your mind, the image will easily weaken, and you will absorb or diffuse yourself into the surrounding stimuli and distractions that will always be present in some form or another. It is best to give a short, quick flashing of the

image onto the other person's eyes at the onset of your interaction. If you fail to obtain or see how the image connects with the other person instantly, then your objectivity will be compromised. It is better to disengage and begin over again to create a strong, clear image in your mind.

BEING TOTALLY OBJECTIVE

Do not question, intellectualize, doubt, or ponder what you perceive; simply absorb to the nth degree; be still, determined, focused and calm. You will see, that to your surprise a dimension of perception will reveal itself to you that you were not expecting. Continue to maintain the image on the person's face before you, repeating the question in your mind-what is your humanity, until it is appropriate to stop. When interfacing with whomever, hold no preconceived notion of what it is that you expect to see. You have no interest or motive one way of another. You simply seek the truth, absorb the truth, and as such, your ray of laser-light perception will penetrate to the core, to the essence of the character and nature of the attribute that you are evaluating in the moment.

To change ourselves effectively,

we first had to change our perceptions.

-STEPHEN R. COVEY, THE 7 HABITS OF HIGHLY
EFFECTIVE PEOPLE: POWERFUL LESSONS IN
PERSONAL CHANGE

YOUR ACTING AS THE ENVIRONMENT

In general, one is easily influenced by their immediate environment where their serenity in one moment can become transitioned to the rough seas of calamity in the next. Any number of contributing factors can come into play, which help to create a change in one's condition/behavior in the moment. You as an evaluator can work as an environmental stimulus, inducing an influence on the person before you. Such a stimulus is the key to uncovering, to breaking open the cover, so to speak, that one holds as a masquerade, preventing one from seeing the true reality of a manifesting conditional attribute. You can act and say any number of things that will induce a significant response from the person right before you. The tool of your acting as the environment can be a very useful weapon in being able to diagnose a targeted attribute in another person. You, acting as the environment, becomes a practical technique, in detecting hidden underlying aspects of a targeted attribute. Bear in mind that the human range of a pendulum swing is vast and huge in its range. Never underestimate the potential inherent range of emotion, behavior, and thoughts that one is capable of manifesting at any moment when one is confronted with a wide range of possible stimulating conditions.

One such example appeared before me on the bus one day. Seated across from me lay bare the hardness and stern look of a middle-aged woman. "What is you joy" was the category attribute that I was intensely engaged upon with the woman sitting across from me; what joy there was at that moment in time was absent in its manifestation. The image of joy did not resonate to a likeness of such when placed over the face of the woman seated across from me. **Then** suddenly change was about to take place. Another woman carrying a very cute young baby boarded the bus. I continued my intense focus upon the woman across from me. Beauty emerged from the woman before me, who was bringing forth a radiance of softness and love. It was at this point that I realized something universal about human life; we cannot make a superficial judgment about the character, personality, or nature of an individual being absolute. We all have the capacity and potential to manifest any number of qualities at any one time. The range of the human condition is vast and expansive, and so our own life can change and move into the positive direction of beauty.

The challenge however, is to shift our pendulum's resting point outward beyond the scope of our self-imposed limitation.

TUNING INTO A CHANNEL

You can become a fine-tuned receiver, capable of resonating to the nature of an attribute. A radio or TV can fine-tune to any number of different channels. We could speak of the different channels as being different attributes, each operating at a stated frequency. You as an evaluator are operating as a receiver, like the TV or radio. Each attribute that we seek to focus upon has its own unique character, its own life, so to speak. The image of the targeted attribute that we have conjured up in our mind will penetrate to the core of its manifesting nature; resonating and meshing with the manifestation of the targeted person in the now moment. You will see for example, the power and influence that the targeted attribute plays in the life of the person before you. Because you are specifically tuned to a given attribute, then as such, you are not fine-tuned to other attributes at the same time. However, overlaps exist between attributes, where there is a commonality of characteristic linkage, and because of that, additional insights into other attributes becomes possible. Your adeptness and speed of discernment will naturally strengthen over time.

RHYTHM

Along with tuning yourself to the nature of an attribute, there becomes your own rhythm of accompaniment. Your rhythm-the way of proceeding in your movement, both physical and mental-is not the same as that of others. By moving into your own sense of rhythm and intuition, you align to what works best, in the moment of your engagement toward others. For example, being in rhythm with music brings us to enjoy and feel the pulse and tempo of a music piece. Sport, too, has rhythm of technique and movement. When you are fined-tuned, objective, focused, and motivated, you will naturally develop a rhythm of coordinated speed so that you are able to generate a capacity to instantly read people. In fact, you can become so proficient in your scanning, that you can view an audience and get instant detection on any attribute that you are targeting, picking out people exhibiting either a positive or negative aspect of an attribute, or anywhere in between. It is something like speed-reading in which you are scanning to find subject matter. Riding on this rhythmic focused scanning enables you to spot the dynamics of change that occurs every moment.

You must live in the present, launch yourself on every

wave, find your eternity in each moment.

-HENRY DAVID THOREAU

It does not matter how slowly you go

as long as you do not stop.

-CONFUCIUS

Here is a list of all ten categories that I have used and suggest:

1) Humanity
2) Stability (how stable is the person?)
3) Joy (what is the person's joy?)
4) Positive (how positive is the person?)
5) Wisdom (to what degree does the person act from wisdom?)
6) Purity (what is the person's purity?)
7) Power source (what is the person's power source?)
8) Perceptual ability (what is the person's perceptual ability?)
9) Connection to the universe (what is the person's connection to the universe?)
10) Respect (what is the person's respect for others?)

MASTER ATTRIBUTE

Since I wrote my first book two years ago, I have come upon, what I would call a master attribute; meaning that there is an attribute/category that I have discovered as being the best and quickest for the evaluation of others. If I were to choose just one attribute to work with, then I would choose the following one:

BEAUTY

Yes, what is your beauty?

• Beauty entails all that there is

• Beauty is a manifestation of many attributes, such as:

One's purity

One's wisdom

One's stability

One's respect for others

One's humanity

One's joy

One's positivity

One's power source

One's connection to the universe, and

One's perceptual ability

... The list goes on-you can add to my list.

. **So,** in one shot of a focused vision, instant penetration, becomes your ally of discovery.

. The focused image of beauty will lead you into a higher realm of consciousness.

. Beauty is not only skin deep, but like Beauty and the Beast, lays deep within one's heart.

. Beauty is consistent from beginning to end in all phenomena.

. Beauty, like a polished mirror, reflects the inner and outer appearances, appearing before it.

. Striving for beauty in your life, will only add to your perception of others.

. Beauty comes in many forms.

How you conjure up the image of beauty, is up to you. Let beauty be your guide, to the x-ray penetration of discovery into others. Beauty is the eternal wellspring of life itself, that pulsates all around us. Once you discover beauty, and produce an image of beauty, then you are on your way in becoming a master of perception.

Beauty is the beauty of life.

It is sunshine.

It is the smile of a child,

the love of a mother,

the joy of a father,

the togetherness of a family.

It is the advancement of humankind,

the victory of a just cause,

the triumph of truth.

-MENACHEIM BEGIN

CONCLUDING THE FIRST STEP

Congratulations on following the trail of this book. You are now ready to begin the implementation of Critical Intent.

It may seem to you that the learning and training of BEV is unrelated to the application of the focused intent of caring for others. But let me say, that unless we know what to look for, perceptually, we will always be ineffective in dynamically producing a move toward our own personal application of Critical Intent, and as such, will fail to grab the dark horse by the tail. In other words, we will flounder about, not seizing the beast of darkness, the sinister workings of delusion and ignorance that currently pervade the lives of so many in today's societies. And consequently, in not calling a spade a spade, we will miss the opportunity in stopping one individual at a time-one individual who can either propel beauty or propel darkness.

Until the great mass of the people shall be filled with

the sense of responsibility for each other's welfare,

Social justice can never be attained.

-HELEN KELLER

PART THREE

Critical Intent & Bull's-eye Vision Together

There are things known and there are things unknown,

and in between are the doors of perception.

-ALDOUS HUXLEY

MY EARLIER DOG experience put together in one moment both Critical Intent and Bull's-eye vision. In putting the two together, I felt and thought of the following during the time of realization:

I was on cloud nine, so to speak, I felt that I had now found a path of direction that I could confidently follow from then on. Incredibly, I could use all the work that had gone into BEV in the past and use it from then on in applying its principles and technique to a greater purpose. Bev was now not relegated to a dusty relic of former limited value but was now in the living construction of value creation. BEV was now fundamental in supporting and maintaining the ongoing conquest to victoriously cut through the darkness, passivity, and isolation that plagues our society today. It's a tool of practical deliverance that anyone can live with moment to moment in daily life. It is not difficult and ephemeral. BEV, together with the directed focused intent in caring for the person before you, at that point, was a working engagement of useful deliverance into the depths of life itself-into the beautiful, creative harmony that permeates all life. All life balances itself to the harmony of creative love, but not necessarily so, for there are those who choose to continue living in their deluded, self-centered space of isolated separation from one another.

You now have as your newfound weapons: Critical Intent and Bull's-eye vision. Because you have walked the path during the course of your life as a person with limited visionary perception, a person with little or no consideration for the necessity of having a focused intent on caring for the person before you, you now need to walk the path of critical deliverance to those whom you will now encounter during the course of your life. Pick up your weapons of choice, march into the fray of your beholding, and make a difference, make an impact that is you, that is who you are now, and that is who you are moment to moment. When you come to the realization that your every moment counts in the direction and condition or your life, and that practicing Critical Intent is the vehicle upon which you can ride throughout your life to experience joy, harmony, and peace within yourself and others, then you will be in a position to exercise the energy of your being to, as my poem touches upon, help someone else:

Generating with my whole being

Gathering up the energies of my soul

In commanding the focus of my mind

My mind and heart infusing to the heart of another.

When you show deep empathy toward others, their

defensive energy goes down, and positive energy

replaces it. That's when you can get more creative in

Solving problems.

-STEPHEN COVEY

BREAKING DOWN THE TWO TOGETHER

Focused Intent: These two words signify **1) Focused-Bull's-eye vision**

2) Intent-Critical Intent

The catch all phrase of "caring for others", sounds nice, but is effectively almost meaningless.

Without focus, direction and action, we will remain in the mental state of niceness.

Focus has energy and power, like a laser beam that is direct, straight, and undiluted. Just having a general idea of caring for others will not penetrate throughout another person's life that is before you; it's not enough of a casual input to ignite and produce a transformation.

Most people have no idea of the giant capacity we

can immediately command when we focus all of our

resources on mastering a single area of our lives.

-TONY ROBBINS

FOCUS AS IT RELATES TO CRITICAL INTENT

Let's go back to my dog experience and the comparative connection that I made at the time as it relates to **Bull's-eye vision** and **Critical Intent.**

From now on, I said to myself, for whomever crosses my path, I will generate with my whole being the focused intent of caring for that person. I determined to train my mind, to focus and seek out, like a laser beam type of vision, to perceive the aspect of caring for others. I was riding the laser beam of a focused intent of caring for the person before me. I was going to implant, pour into the person before me, a love of caring, concern and touching. I would mesh and connect with the person before me to the deepest level that my laser beam focus would take me.

Focus, in the case of applying **Critical Intent,** has two aspects/components:

1) Creating a clear image of something. As was presented in **Bull's-eye vision,** we exercised our mind to create an image for a specific category/aspect, whether it was humanity, anger, purity, etc. Once we had created a clear image of a specific category/aspect, then we took the second step.

2) Directing and maintaining the created image, via a laser beam toward the person at hand.

3) The difference between the focus of **BEV** and the focus of Critical Intent is that in **BEV**, you are focusing on seeking out/evaluating what is the manifesting condition of a targeted aspect/category trait in the person before you. In the case of Critical Intent, you are not seeking, or extracting out a targeted trait/aspect about the person before you, but you are reversing the focus rather than from extraction, but to one of implantation of the image, or pouring of the image onto the person before you.

So, in the case of Critical Intent, you have created an image of what you visualize as caring, love, or concern for another person. Your intent at the same time is in tune with, one with, the image of caring that you have created. As I said in the poem that I wrote, "My mind and heart infusing to the heart of another. My heart meshes into the heart of others." The focused image of caring immediately penetrates through the icy darkness in people's lives, like in the poem:

"Like a laser beam of clarity

I perceive the darkness

The bastion of resistance

That cannot hide from the shining light of a caring heart.

My heart meshes into

the heart of others."

So, the practice and training of **BEV** allows you to effectively direct and place your strong laser beam of a focused intent into the life of another. The physics of life's workings produces a positive change in your immediate environment because you have successfully causally inputted the necessary ingredients needed to produce the desired effect of making a positive transformation, or movement, to take place between you and the person before you.

So, the two, **Bull's-eye vision** and **Critical Intent,** both work together simultaneously to allow an opening whereupon another person's life becomes touched by the light of a caring heart, and thereby the seed of such is planted; as stated in my poem:

"As we part

The seed of a caring intent has been planted

May the water and nutrition that you so inherently hold

Begin to nurture and grow

So that you may glow

To become the person

Who everybody knows.

Its not what you look at that matters, its what you see.

-HENRY DAVID THOREAU

MASTER FOCUS

What is your master focus? What is the one image of focused intent that you would call your most effective and valuable focus? Amongst all your possible focused images of intent that you have engaged in and will do so in the future, there is one that packs in the most concentrated value of benefit to your life; a perceptual image that rises above others in a way that could be described as standing on the highest mountain over looking all other mountains in a vast terrain that we call life. The master focused image of the "Focused Intent on Caring for others," is the Master Focus that will lead you into the depths of life itself; into the depths of a person's heart.

You could talk about the frequency vibration of a focused image, the inherent qualities of such, and its affect on others and the environment. A scientific measuring device could be used to detect and measure the specifications of different image vibrations. There is one such study/experiment worthy of mention, summarized briefly in the following:

Meditation Study-8 weeks to a better Harvard 2011

Brief Summary of Mindfulness Research

Greg Flaxman and Lisa Flook, Ph.D.

Researchers' interest in mindfulness practice has steadily increased as studies continue to reveal its beneficial effects. Current research looks at how the brain responds to mindfulness practice, how relationships benefit, and how physical and mental health improves, as well as other topics. The following presents a sample of the results from investigations seeking to uncover more of what mindfulness can offer to enhance human well-being.

Brain & Immune System

A burgeoning field of study has grown out of interest for the effects of mindfulness practice on the brain. Current literature points towards the potential for mindfulness to affect the structure and neural patterns present in the brain. Scientists have seen these results last not only during mindfulness practice, but also during the daily life of practitioners. The results of one study published in NeuroReport in 2005 show thicker cortical regions related to attention and sensory processing in long-term meditation practitioners compared to non-meditators. These findings also suggest that meditation practice may offset cortical thinning brought on by aging1.

A recent study outlines the difference in neural functions related to emotion in expert meditators and novice meditators. Individuals performed compassion meditations, while researchers measured how the regions in the brain responsible for emotion regulation reacted to varying stimuli.

The more advanced meditators showed more activation in those areas of the brain that detect emotional cues, demonstrating a heightened empathic awareness2.

However, not all studies involve expert meditators. A 2003 study focused on how an 8-week training course would affect the brains and immune systems of individuals. This investigation provided some evidence of increased activation in a region of the brain correlated with positive affect, as well as evidence that the immune system would react more robustly in antibody production after meditation training3.

Another recent study showed better stress regulation, as measured by a faster decrease in levels of the stress hormone cortisol following a stressful laboratory task, among Chinese undergraduates after 5 days of meditation training at 20 minutes a day. These students also reported less anxiety, depression, and anger compared to a group of students that received relaxation training4.

Relationships

Mindfulness training may affect an individual's ability to harbor successful social relationships as well. A University of North Carolina at Chapel Hill study demonstrated a correlation between mindfulness practice in couples and an enhanced relationship. The couples reported improved closeness, acceptance of one another, autonomy, and general relationship satisfaction5.

A 2007 study replicated this finding, also demonstrating a correlation between mindfulness and quality of communication between romantic partners6. Loving-kindness meditation, which can involve positive imagery or wishes directed toward others or self, can affect how one relates to others. A recent study examined how individuals reacted to viewing photographs of strangers after loving kindness meditation. The meditation significantly affected the positive values they attributed to those strangers, demonstrating a relationship between loving-kindness meditation and social connectedness7.

Mindfulness practice can benefit familial relationships. Parents of children with developmental disabilities described increased satisfaction with their parenting, more social interactions with their children, and less parenting stress as a result of mindfulness training8.

In another study carried out by the same researchers regarding parents of children with autism, the same results of increased satisfaction in their parenting skills and relationship applied9.

In both studies, the children of these parents benefited from the mindful parenting practice, showing decreases in aggressive and non-compliant behavior.

In addition, a mindfulness intervention for adolescents with externalizing disorders that involved their parents in the treatment showed improvement in the happiness of the children, as well as the parents' perception of their child's self-control10.

Clinical

A popular form of mindfulness intervention, devised by Jon Kabat-Zinn, is Mindfulness-Based Stress Reduction (MBSR). This intervention originally came about to help those with chronic pain issues or stress-related disorders. Typically in MBSR programs, individuals go through an 8-10 week session in which they practice for at least 45 minutes a day.

Numerous therapies incorporating mindfulness have sprouted in recent years. Mindfulness-based cognitive therapy, similar to MBSR, teaches individuals to recognize their thoughts and feelings with a nonjudgmental attitude. When researchers studied its effectiveness in preventing a relapse of depression for those in remittance from a depressive episode, 37% of those that went through an 8-week MBCT program experienced a relapse compared to 66% of those not in the program11.

Helping professionals can use mindfulness to improve their abilitiy to empathize with those they serve as well. A study of an 8-week MBSR course for nurses showed that their mindfulness practice facilitated empathic attitudes, as well as decreased their tendency to take on others' negative emotions12.

A previous study of health-care professionals going through the 8-week MBSR program presented results of increased self-compassion and reduced stress in those individuals13. Such self-care may trickle down to improve upon the quality of the relationship between those professionals and their clients.

While the majority of mindfulness studies have focused on adults, some pertain to the practice of mindfulness in children and adolescents. A series of studies have documented its use as an intervention for youth with psychological disturbances. In one 6-week study with anxious children, teachers reported an improvement in academic functioning and decrease in symptoms of anxiety in the children14.

Another utilized mindfulness-based cognitive therapy with the result of significantly reducing observable internalizing and externalizing symptoms. Over 80% of children and parents involved in this study thought that schools should teach mindfulness15. A mindfulness intervention for several adolescents with conduct disorder resulted in a significant decrease in aggressive behavior. They reported benefits from mindfully returning their attention to the soles of their feet during distressing situations16. In a recent study for adolescents with ADHD, mindfulness training significantly reduced symptoms associated with their disorder17.

Education

There is increasing interest in the utility of mindfulness practices in educational settings. A study of 1st-3rd grade children that involved a 12-week program of breath awareness and yoga (delivered once per week every other week) showed improvements in children's attention and social skills as well as decreased test anxiety in children who went through the training as compared to controls18. Another program that combined elements of MBSR and tai chi for a small group of middle school students in a 5-week program found that students reported an increased sense of calm, connection to nature, and improved sleep after going through the training19.

Two pilot studies conducted through UCLA's Mindful Awareness Research Center indicate improvements in self regulatory abilities among preschool and elementary school students who participated in an 8-week mindful awareness practices training program (developed and taught by InnerKids in two 30-minute sessions per week). Specifically, children who were initially less well-regulated showed the strongest improvements subsequent to training, as compared to children in the control group who did not receive the training20 21.

These preliminary findings suggest potential benefit and practical applications of mindfulness for children in school settings.

Other mind/body practices

Mindfulness is not alone in the world of mind/body awareness practices currently studied by scientists. A 2006 qualitative study followed the effects of one year of Transcendental Meditation™ (during the first and last 10 minutes of each school day) on ten middle school students. Themes that emerged from individual interviews with students included a greater ability at self-control and improved social relationships, as well as better academic performance. Other investigators have evaluated the benefits of Yoga as well22. Investigators found Sahaja Yoga Meditation, an awareness practice related to mindfulness, as an effective intervention for children with ADHD and their families. Results included an improvement in the self-esteem of the children, a reduction in their ADHD symptoms, and an improved relationship between parent and child23.

A study of Iyengar Yoga as a complement to medication in the treatment of depression found significant reductions in overall depression, anger, and anxiety among participants. Participants also consistently rated their moods higher after the completion of each class than before each one commenced24. The underlying mechanisms involved in these types of practice remain to be understood, although it appears that each does offer health benefits.

While the discussed research gives one a glimpse into the many topics of study involving mindfulness, it does not capture the complete picture. Some areas have barely been broached by investigators, including mindfulness in the workplace and mindfulness in athletics. Future investigations may increasingly shed light on both how mindfulness works as well as directly comparing various forms of practice.

1 Lazar, S., et al. (2005). Meditation experience is associated with increased cortical thickness. NeuroReport, 16(17), 1893-1897.

2 Lutz, A., et al. (2008). Regulation of the Neural Circuitry of Emotion by Compassion Meditation: Effects of Meditative Expertise. PLoS One, 3(3), 1-10.

3 Davidson, R., et al. (2003). Alterations in Brain and Immune Function Produced by Mindfulness Meditation. Psychosomatic Medicine, 65, 564-570.

4 Tang, Y., et al. (2007). Short-term meditation training improves attention and self-regulation. PNAS, 104(43), 17152-17156.

5 Carson, J., et al. (2004). Mindfulness-Based Relationship Enhancement. Behavior Therapy, 35, 471-494.

6 Barnes, S., et al. (2007). The role of mindfulness in romantic relationship satisfaction and response to relationship stress. Journal of Marital and Family Therapy, 33(4), 482-500.

Nevertheless, through my personal experience with focusing on a multitude of focused intent images, I can say that the one imaged focus that has worked at being the most powerful and effective for me is the focused intent image of "The Focused Intent of caring for the person that crosses one's path moment to moment." Why, what facts are there to support such a conclusion?

1) "Strengthening your framework"

Individuals who operate from their framework of operation, set themselves up to move ahead in their life one way or another. For example: What is your journey's vision-goals/dreams? Moving forward in our vision/purpose requires a structured base from which our life operates and moves forward. Within our framework, you could define various essential components as being necessary in achieving our goals. For example: We need a physical body and mind to function, requiring effort in maintaining such. Financial resources of some kind are required. Our attitude will have a bearing on our outcomes and victory in life. As well, we need careful, organized and systematic planning in our movement forward toward our goals. And the one essential ingredient, the master ingredient, if you will, is the component of having the focused intent in caring for others. we are, for example being constantly targeted indiscriminately by medias outreach of negative news coverage reporting. A climate of insincerity, greed, self centered materialism, hatred, and anger to name only a few pervade our every moment. Having peace and tranquility in our life comes about with the practice of having "the focused intent of caring for others who cross our path moment to moment." This focused intent of caring for others, needs to be an essential component built into our structure, without which, we will fall prey to our own inherent negative and destructive forces, sabotaging an already weakened structure.

2) Master of all images

We have learned that we can conceptualize a wide range of focused images, that when placed over the face of individuals, can reveal instantly a huge array of insights and readings from the targeted attribute that we are evaluating from the individual in question before us. We have also learned that there is an overlap between certain focused images, that because of their similar nature, can and do offer insights and readings encompassing other attributes. For example, let's say that our focused image category/attribute is asking, what is your purity (not your purity, but the person whom you are evaluating.) You will find and see that the aspect of your conceptualized image of purity, will also include, trustworthiness, reliability, honesty, and loyalty to name a few.

The focused image of Critical Intent functions as what I call a Mater image, that can also detect other manifesting attributes emanating from an individual close at hand. Since Critical Intent directs the focus of a loving and caring heart onto another individual in front of us, the aspect of evaluation is of a secondary function and consequence. However interestingly I have found that, by matter of the nature of applying Critical Intent, we naturally are able to detect a huge range of manifesting attribute conditions, from the person in question. Although our purpose of Critical Intent is not to evaluate as in the case of BEV, we find that we are still able to gain BEV's resulting benefit.

3) **Most effective, all encompassing image**

The image of Critical Intent at once captures the dark horse by the tail, so to speak. As I mentioned earlier, we our constantly battling a slowing decaying, insidious alienation from the profound aspect of our own humanity. Not to mention the myriad of senseless, meaningless, and negative distractions impinging upon us every moment. The antidote to our effective and value creating posture for not only ourselves, but also for others is our practice of Critical Intent every moment. This practice, Critical Intent, at once raises our life condition higher, that by itself, shatters the dark hold of our default position, be it, anger, sadness, negativity, anxiousness, jealously, and so on into the vicious dark hole of our falling. The realm or condition of Critical Intent is the light of our caring heart, the unfolding of our connective senses to all that surrounds us, and the confidence, wisdom, compassion, and effective touching of others that will be in the moment of our shining best self. Other focusing images, of course have great value, and there is a place and time to their application. But if I were to choose only one focused image as being our default, it would be the focus of Critical Intent.

APPLYING CRITICAL INTENT TO ONESELF

Applying Critical Intent to oneself, reinforces one's inner state of life that allows a readiness of strength in dealing with anything that may come one's way. For example, you may come across someone who, for whatever reason, gives you an unpleasant look. Depending on your conditional state, how you filter and respond to such an outside stimulus, is your indicator gauge of your inner strength. Without a strong inner self, you will be at the mercy of the inner workings of a weak self. Such a weak self, will implode upon itself, and as such, practicing Critical Intent for others will be compromised; better to regroup and renew yourself in applying Critical Intent to yourself. Establishing a strong inner self by giving love, honour, and blessing to every part of your being, will give you the needed inner strength of confidence and courage. Be the lion that you are, never giving into cowardice, and be the shinning light of caring that you naturally behold in the depths of your life.

   As in creating an image that we used in our application of **BEV**, formulate whatever imagery works for you-could be white light infusing and showering your whole being; could be water, energy, or just the image of love filling your cup. Do not forget to remind yourself that at times of weakness, depression, upset, or self torturing anger, to once again fill up your cup. Critical Intent is there for your refill-use it! Be balanced, both for your own Critical Intent of self, and for that of others.

Physical Health

Common sense dictates our well being in the arena of physical health. As such, giving our body good nutrition, sufficient rest and exercise, are basic requirements for optimal functioning of applying Critical Intent. See a Doctor whenever the occasion warrants. I have personally seen too many people in putting off seeing a Doctor, only to be told later by a Physician, "why did you wait so long."

When we develop a strong solid self, and address the well being of our physical health, then Critical Intent will be our sharp sword that cuts through the entanglements and darkness that pervades people's lives today. Make a difference to both yourself and others. Awaken to your own power, and boldly walk forth into the fray of your unique glorious mission.

It is during our darkest moments that we

must focus to see the light.

-ARISTOTLE ONASSIS

A GIFT OF YOUR OWN TAKING

You have now been given a gift that is yours to take. Take it; its yours for the keeping. Please remember to honor your fellow human being who surrounds your every moment. You are a unique individual, and only you can implement a way toward a better life for yourself. I have offered you a way forward, a way of perceiving life, and a consideration to a different way of being present for others. The task is not easy in the sense that one cannot assume that you have the desired intent to care for others. What does it take for you to care for others? When you come to the realization that caring for others, is at the same time caring for yourself-for your eternal future, then you can claim the right to be of the highest status in life, regardless of what position you hold.

Remember a real decision is measured by the fact that you've taken new action. If there's no action, you haven't Truly decided.

-TONY ROBBINS

PART FOUR

MY STORY

THIS NOW LEADS YOU to my story, to my journey to the point of recognizing and accepting that the focused intent of caring for others is the answer to the correct way of life, or less absolute, to a better way of life.

My life is not better, any more special, or remarkable that that of anyone else. My story is not about touting the superiority of what I have to say. I simply want to tell you what I went through to come to this point of my life, which I feel is important to tell so that others can benefit from my story. I believe that my story has a purpose in relating to others' personal experiences.

Your experience is an untold story that you alone have withstood. I share with you the quietness of your enduring witness to a life of uniqueness, wonder, and adventure. Tucked between your joy and sorrow, relief and suffering, is your story, which is not one of waste. Your story has purpose and meaning within the intricacy of a complex and meandering life. To the degree and extent that we overlap in our experiences of significance, the question is whether we can pull together meaning and purpose that will lead you to adopting the value of "Critical Intent." My story is not an attempt to display an entertaining story of nonfiction fascination or to impress you with a clever composition of storytelling, but simply to help **break open the refusal, blindness, and immovable stubbornness that the dark side of our life entails; they are elements that rein over our everyday thoughts and actions.**

EARLY BEGINNINGS

BORN INTO A protective environment that allowed me to live in security and opportunity for physical, intellectual, and spiritual growth, I found Toronto, a place of relative calm and peace. Ours was a place that provided easy access to schools, parks, hospitals, and commercial services.

By many standards, ours was a privileged class that enjoyed an ease to life that most people in this world could not afford. It was a normal early primary school life by most standards, and it was uncomplicated as I advanced in development across an array of areas such as education, sports, religion, and family.

After primary school, all of us children left the public school system to enrol in the private school system. Both my brother and I attended a prestigious boys private boarding school, famous for hosting Prince Andrew of England as one of the boys attending the school, while my two sisters stayed in Toronto as day students to attend an all-girls school for day students and private boarding students. We all experienced a curriculum of balanced academics, sports, social activities, compulsory chapel, and relative freedom to pursue hobbies of interest.

Out of our primary and secondary school years, in the protective environment that we found ourselves, we all proceeded on to the universities of our choices. Let me summarize the important points, during this part of my life, as they relate to Critical Intent.

The carefree living and openness that afforded me a comfortable upbringing was, by itself, just that. The underpinnings that permeate people's lives and society, on the other hand, are notable in the context of a society immersed in a culture of passive acceptance. Passive acceptance of what, you ask? This is the point of reference, the platform upon which I will attempt to address that question.

NOT ON THE RADAR

WE GROW UP and are shielded and misdirected from the essential necessity of living our daily life, in developing ourselves fully in the mindful struggle to care for others. I don't mean in the sense of charity-not to negate the value of it, but I mean to be mindful and directive to, a priori, the given of a constant battle within ourselves. That battle is to fight and win over the human tendency to concentrate and lie back into the self-centered pursuit of solely benefiting ourselves-be it through material, educational, status, or power-based acquisition-while neglecting to engage the force of our life in living for the benefit and happiness of others.

"Not on the radar" is indicative of a catch phrase that captures the limiting of our life to a compliant fixation of filtering out that which is perceived as non-important to the pursuit of what we value as being the route and path of our striving destination. Oblivious to the realm of caring, we carry on our lives in the way we do. Shielded from the aging and progression of our lives, we comfort ourselves in the veil of ignorance. We get by in not considering where the radar of our lives and that of society do not detect, register, or consider the following critical thought: a focused intent of caring for others is actually critical for our lives, for our final tally in life that registers and measures our humanistic actions for our fellow human beings. We march toward death surrounded by the veil of ignorance, content to revel in our accomplishments of self, but in the end it's too late to turn back the clock; the clock of life has expired, and we failed to realize our great capacity and essence, to have released and exploded forth the beauty that we so inherently hold. The essential beauty and love of our life is to reach out to others, to hold fast our brethren, to walk together with those of our common liking-a liking of being one with others from where we came and to where we are bound. Regardless of a dividing culture and religion, we cannot escape the reality of life, the workings of life itself. The pulsation of creation and love that permeates life and the universe is there for the taking. However blind we may have become to such, it becomes our loss, our unfortunate waste, where the bypass exit that we have chosen will lead us to where we did not have to be.

So be it; that is the way that we have come to know. That is the way we have been taught both in our schooling and upbringing. Little consideration has been given to the notion of generating a mindset conducive to proactive engagement toward others' happiness. In our wake, we disperse through life, flooding our mind and body with the acquisition of material treasures and the development of our body and mind to live out the fulfillment of our perceived values-values that have little to do with the happiness of others outside our family, close friends and relatives.

Enjoy life, yes, strive to obtain the material things that give you pleasure. Work and study hard to master your skills and profession. Aim for that goal and target of a better career, of a better station in life. Money is fine; enjoy its practical use, and if you need more of it, then go for it. But do not lead a life devoid of the balanced necessity, because an ongoing intent for the well-being of others is critical for the advancement of our life to one of greatness, to a life that shines with humanity. You can have both, the material fruits of enjoyment and necessity, and the fruits and blessings of the nonmaterial that will enable you to be a person of the highest status, to be a person who others will marvel at because you will glow with richness in all aspects of your life.

Rather than love, than money, than fame, give me truth.

-HENRY DAVID THOREAU

Rare is the man who seeks not only to heal

himself but to heal his fellow man.

-JOSE' N. HARRIS, MI VIDA

If all you do is look out for yourself, then…you're not

really looking out for yourself.

Taking care of those that love and care about you is

Critical. Living just for yourself is not really living.

I'm a Scientist. Its not only a beautiful and rewarding

Way to go through life, it's also Darwinian!"

-JOSE' N. HARRIS, MI VIDA

FLOUNERING TIMES

BACK AGAIN IN the midst of my journey, I was a person who was seeking to improve myself both in terms of career and spiritually. Although I was seeking a so-called "enlightenment," it was always illusive. I tried Transcendental Meditation in the hope of achieving a so-called "cosmic consciousness," but even though there was benefit to the discipline of the meditation, I was being very much governed by the inner workings of my dark side. I faced a daily struggle of the path toward goodness and purity versus a decline into addictive obsessions that were consuming and taking over my life bit my bit. I struggled with this battle of darkness for twenty years before I was in control again and had won against two major addictions. In between these years I had other addictions, but by some standards they were more acceptable. I studied all the books I could find on how to make money playing at casinos. I took many trips to Atlantic City and Las Vegas to try my luck. In the end I was out of luck and out of money. My conclusion was that you cannot beat the house advantage in the long run. You may be lucky and win in the short term, but if you play long enough, you will eventually lose. However, hats off to those blackjack players who have been barred from casinos.

Another addiction that I developed was online chess, which took up vast amounts of my time and created much misery in our house when I would swear loudly when I lost a game or made a bad move. No matter how I explained to my wife that I was only voicing at that moment, and then I was OK, she could not accept or understand it. My three children as well were greatly affected negatively by my continued online chess playing. My eldest daughter, felt that I had abandoned her, forgotten her, as I became lost in the online gaming world. Due, to my many addictions and distractions, I did not graduate from university until twenty years after I entered my first year. Although I never gave up and finally graduated, I found myself with a general BA degree that did not give me an automatic passage into the job field that I had studied.

All the obsessive addictions that I encountered were ways to slow down my advancement to a better place spiritually. But I never gave up; I always knew that somehow, some day I would overcome my addictions and be clear of such. Time, though, did not wait; time marches on, and it seemed that there was not much time left, as we naturally age.

My first significant brush with what you might call touching the realm of love that pervades the universe happened sixteen years ago when I experienced a heart attack. The plaque in my right coronary artery ruptured and formed a blood clot, blocking my right coronary artery 100%.

What was interesting and meaningful was that during the same morning of my heart attack, I was chanting/praying very strongly and determined to break open my karma, to break open the impediments in my life that were holding me back, that were blocking me from breaking free from constraints that held my life down from advancing to be a better person. I visualized that my chanting was like the crashing waves against a solid, immovable rock and that it would eventually change the shape of the rock over time.

I was determined to impact my karma in a way that would allow me to move forward without the karmic restraints that I had somehow created through the thoughts and actions of my life. I did feel the force of my chanting making an impact somewhere in my life as it related to my karma.

Two hours later I had the heart attack while playing badminton against my son up at my mother's cottage. Incredibly, I did not even consider that I was having a heart attack. In fact, I took the strange symptoms as indicating that I was out of shape, so I continued to play badminton. A week later, while back at home in Toronto, it occurred to me that I might have some blockage in my arteries. A trip to the Doctor and an electrocardiogram reading confirmed that I indeed had had a heart attack, and off to the hospital I went.

Incredibly, the angiogram test revealed that, yes, my right coronary artery was 100% blocked, and my left coronary artery was 40% blocked. The angiogram also revealed that I had amazingly developed collateral blood vessels that provided an alternate supply of blood to my heart. Even though part of my heart tissue had died from insufficient blood flow to my heart, I walked out of the hospital with minimal heart damage and was able to function normally with no disability.

During my stay in the hospital, I experienced an overwhelming feeling of gratitude/appreciation for the whole event that had taken place. I had been protected and supported by life itself. I could feel the love, protection, and support all around me. I felt the incredible loving force from something outside and within my life. I felt a oneness with the cosmos, a loving embrace that signaled to me that we are not alone, that there is a loving force always with us, and that living with gratitude is one of the key elements that we need to live with moment to moment if we want to open up the gateway to a greater self that expands beyond the confines of a negative, complaining, and ungrateful smaller self.

So, I find myself now, at this time in my life, having found the key to unlock and open the path to a glorious and fulfilling life. The key, recipe, or formula, if you will, is the discovery that I made through my dog experience-that having the focused intent to care for others moment to moment is critical to our advancement to be the best kind of person that we can be.

Love the moment, and the energy of that moment will

spread beyond boundaries.

-CORITA KENT

PART FIVE

WHY CRITICAL INTENT

Better World and Environment

What can we do as an individual to make for a better world? All of us in some way or another contribute to the betterment of the place or surroundings in which we live, and an such will impact the world at large. If we consider the physical workings-ripple effect-butterfly effect that life produces, a positive change in one individual will naturally in turn impact another individual, and that individual will impact others, and so on. However, the question is, what positive changes constitute a changed individual? Getting back to practicing Critical Intent, that inward change of your awakening to the focused intent of caring for the person(s) in front of you will create the movement toward your evolvement to that place of higher consciousness, purity, and liberation from a self -imposed prison of your self-centered deluded self. The continual practice of Critical Intent will allow the growth of you as a human being, to master your deluded mind to take control over your default position of a self-centered deluded egotistical mind. The continual struggle and battle to reign in the tendency of our reactive self that gravitates towards, negative impulsive actions and behaviors will begin the strength and sustainability in maintaining Critical Intent moment to moment. And the change taking place in you, will spread to impact others, and in turn will impact your immediate environment, and in turn affect the larger environment surrounding you. A better world starts with each of us becoming a person of humanity, and together with our fellow humans uniting as differing culturally divergent individuals, contributing to the self-awakened goal of happiness and peace for all citizens of this planet.

On another vital topic that concerns us all is that of our next life, and the future generations of our heritage. The workings of life do not stop when we pass away. What you have done in the past and during your present life, will impact your continuum on into your future existence. And not only you, yourself, but also your family ties now and in the future will be impacted as well from the actions of your life, on into many future generations. Such are the consequence of one's actions in this life upon others. Facts of life, such as science, physics, energy, and karma to name a few, are an indisputable part of our life here on earth. Religion will have its different interpretations about the truth of life, but I only offer my sincere, open and honest view of that which I have seen and experienced during my lifetime.

Individual Happiness

What does it take for us to become happy? That illusive question, like a fuzzy fog that does not come into crystal clear focus. This way or that way, this technique, this attitude, this practice and so on it goes. I'm not here to give a definitive answer, for all have valid suggestions and tips to being happy. However, I can say that a critical component to being happy is engaging in the practice of Critical Intent. Without a concern and care for others outside the umbrella of our family, then the attainment of happiness, is structured like a sandcastle, that does not have the structural strength to withstand the passage of time, or to put it another way, our happiness is as fragile as the morning dew. We must earn our happiness with persevering effort. It takes effort, concentration, training and practice to engage in every possible moment the practice of Critical Intent, but the rewards are far that will naturally impact happiness of self and make a positive impact upon others that cross our path in our daily life.

We understand what we earn

We struggle with what we are given

There is a reason most lottery

Winners become train wrecks

Earn it.

-ALEX CHARFEN

Gaining wisdom, Intuition, and Confidence

The grand partaking of your uplifted spirit into the realm of other's lives has begun a process/movement towards an expanded arena of openness and unity between you and others. As such, the walled divisions and blockages that existed prior to your awakening and growth into becoming a person of humanity, are beginning to crumble and melt away, allowing you now to access wisdom, intuition, and confidence. Wisdom is earned, not an automatic given. Grab the mantle of your humanity that you are now exhibiting, due to your work in practicing Critical Intent, and walk the light of confidence, wisdom and intuition. As natural is the ebb and flow of the ocean, you too can have your moments, your rhythmic cresting of self awareness and interactions into the depths that wisdom, intuition, and confidence have to offer. There is a limitless well, and ongoing stream, that never dries up, when you exercise the moment to moment focused intent in caring for the person(s) who cross your path.

"The saddest aspect of life right now is that science gathers

*gathers knowledge **faster** than society gathers wisdom."*

- ISAAC ASIMOV

Our Attitude

What should our attitude be, when we are talking about practicing Critical Intent? You know, our attitude plays a key role in all aspects of our lives. How we look at the world, internalize what we see, and react to our surroundings, all are integrated within the attitude that we hold at each moment. One moment we can take on a certain attitude, and another moment can maybe tweak our attitude a bit, and other moments can take on a completely different attitude; such is the range of our somewhat complicated and unpredictable self that seems to appear to us in general. However, there are some common threads of consistency that operate within our life, that bear mentioning, as it affects our ability to practice Critical Intent effectively.

Never seek the truth about someone with the attitude that I know it all- you don't know it, because you have not even tried to know and understand with an open and seeking mind to what is presented to you in the present moment. The big mistake is to make assumptions, before you even tried to look objectively at the person before you. As I mentioned before in the topic of Perception, we look at others through tainted glasses, further deluding us as to what we see in front of us. Take off your tainted glasses, take off your masked façade of delusion, and proceed to the checkout with the truth of what you really bring to the register-carrying the attitude of being open in seeking the truth, and having a heart of gold; your focused caring to the brethren of your belonging who walk amongst us, for your eternal advancement into a life of meaning and value.

What to Expect

What are your expectations? You must have some idea of what you can expect in the future to come. Striving for your goals, your step by step planning and movements toward such, and your hopes and desires for all that you are seeking, must enhance a sense of some expectation. However, you will not expect about what I'm about to say.

Grab hold of your armored mantle as you begin to battle the darkness that lies deep in your life, and the darkness that attempts to stop you dead in your tracks, for you are now a person of light, that has decided and determined to step forward into the fray of your awakening. The first step in such an honorable battle, is to recognize that you are fighting a noble cause for justice and the noble awakening of others, to their inherent goodness, to lead a life of fulfillment and happiness; that others, too, will have the focused intent in caring for others. We are all behind you, witnessing and cheering you on, forces and functions throughout life, and of course your life itself, all calling you to take your bold entry into the lives of all who cross your path moment to moment, and they too are seeking your entrance into their life.

You can expect the unexpected. For example, you will find that every day you will learn something new, that either you never thought of before, or will reinforce something that you heard before as being important, but never really internalized into your life. Grow and learn each day, the lessons of your growth and learning will begin to accelerate, and your mind will be filled with rushes of new insights. A bright and shinning vista is opening before you, as you harness the focus of your intent into the lives of others.

Your new encounters with others, becomes a strong, learning and valued mark, in both your life and that of another who crosses your path. In the depths of another's life is a melting pot of positive potential buried beneath their seemingly vacant holding. Be ready to engage and allow the unfolding of their buried treasures to emerge, give the nourishment and water to the fruits of their beholding, listen, be patient and tolerant to their way of expression and coming to and out. Once you have given your all, walk away and know that you have made a cause for the future path to unfold before you.

"Positive expectations are the mark of the superior personality."

- Brian Tracy, Maximum Achievement: Strategies and Skills that Will Unlock Your Hidden Powers to Succeed

"If you're reading this...
Congratulations, you're alive.
If that's not something to smile about,
then I don't know what is."

- Chad Sugg, Monsters Under Your Head

You and Your Environment

You are not a castle or an island by itself but, are interconnected to all that surrounds you. Practicing Critical Intent, begins the tune and vibration that resounds throughout your life and immediate environment. You, as an individual play an integral part in the composition of this alchemic mixing, adding the color and uniqueness of your engaging, charm sounding hue. The illuminating light that shines from you when practicing Critical Intent will spill over into other areas of your life; such is the consistency of Critical Intent's main-stay. For example, besides feeling good about yourself in general, there also is a physiological correspondence within you matching the so called feel good sensation that you feel when practicing Critical Intent. The whereabouts of where your instinctual radar guides you, will lead you into places that match the timing, condition, need, and value of your presence in the moment. Trust in the place that you are in the moment as being a place where purpose, value, good, and beauty are taking place, to create a movement towards a better place, both for you and your environment.

So, what you say, what has this got to do with leading a simple, uncomplicated, and enjoyable life. Let life be what it is, and don't read too much into some abstract theoretical talk that sounds like you are bordering on nonsense talk. Good point I say, and believe me, I have had my fill with hype-bole enigmatic talk. But, I say practice Critical Intent first, and then reread what I have written; practice more, and reread again, then you will see the truth to what I say. I myself am always learning, developing and communicating the essence of what it is that we want others to know. Just know that you, who are unique, will impact others and your environment wherever you go, and that practicing Critical Intent will bring out the best in you and your environment.

Work Place

The place where you work is the place that you spend much of your life. Enjoy or not to enjoy, grow or not to grow, these are the value of your work place. The entity of your work place, in general, exists to be an enterprise of business, in making and sustaining profit. We partake in the company's mandate, being rewarded for our contribution. The tally of our day to day time spent at work provides a memory for our life. The extraction of lessons learned from those memories, provide a basis for spring boarding our life to one of growth and value. Never view your workplace as empty time spent but, see it as a stepping stone to an expanded life, that has yet to reveal its full potential.

A dream doesn't become reality through magic;

it takes sweat, determination and hard work.

- COLIN POWELL

My Own Experiences-Relating to Critical Intent

My work place:

During my twenty-one years working at my present job in Toronto, I have had the opportunity to witness a great transformation at my work place.

Amongst the staff who work at this beautiful high-end building, are a group of us who have worked together side by side for a relatively long period of time. During our many hours of working together, side by side, we have had the opportunity to engage in many interesting discussions of various topics. Over our time together, there has been a gradual change in the type of topics discussed. From the sunshine girl topic at the beginning of my work here, to sport scores, to the weather, and dreaming about how nice it would be to have all those things that we cannot afford.

Then suddenly, starting about seven years ago my colleague at work heard a Philosopher talking on a broadcast, that suddenly struck a chord in his life; a realization took place that began the start of his life to move into a new direction. Since that very moment seven years ago until now, he has become a constant source of wisdom and clarity about things that are important in life for us all. No more small talk about those things that have little value to us becoming a person of humanity. He has written a book, put himself in excellent physical shape, got married and now has two wonderful children, that together with his wife are modeling fine examples of wonderful parents.

Another colleague, with whom I share much in common, has also gone through a similar transformation. We too engaged in common boy's locker room talk and had similar tastes. At the same time though, we both were seeking a way to improve ourselves spiritually. Bit by bit over the years, are discussions were more and more engaged in matters of religion, philosophy, ideas of profound significance as it relates to being humanistic-a person that could contribute to the betterment of humanity. Once I had my dog experience, that I mentioned before, and started writing my first book titled "Critical Intent," things took off exponentially, transforming the both of us in becoming better persons. To this day, the three of us are on our own journey, in the pursuit of our own development, sharing with others wherever we can, and leading much more fulfilling and happier lives.

My Neglect of Practicing Critical Intent

Sustaining Critical Intent has its own inherent weaknesses that invades all of us at some point. Being human brings forth its own aspects of laziness and neglect. Whatever the case may be, I too found myself neglecting the practice of Critical Intent, even though I had written a book about it.

   One day my neglect of practicing Critical Intent, came to a head, with the following experience: I was driving by a construction site one day when I came upon a Construction Worker who was holding up a stop sign, helping to guide traffic through a busy intersection. He was waving his hand, motioning me to proceed slowly ahead, but at the same time, still holding up the stop sign. Suddenly he banged his stop sign up and down, yelling at me to **STOP, STOP, STOP!!** Because I had a previous run in with this person a couple of weeks prior, I anticipated that something might again happen, but not to the extent that was about to take place. I rolled down my car window yelling at him that I was only following his directions. He loudly shouted back saying that he only directed me to move straight ahead and not to the right. In my reactionary anger, I asked him what his name was, which just seemed to antagonize him further, as he walked back shaking his head, as if I was a nut case. Then I just lost it, yelling at him as hard as I could, "you don't have to f…g yell at me that way."-he just shook his head and told me to get the hell out of here. Initially, I felt both relieved and agitated at the same time; relieved, because I knew that if I had said nothing, it would have eaten me up inside. After calming down somewhat and reflecting on what had just transpired, I came to the realization, that I had lately, not been practicing Critical Intent. This event shook the core of my mindless forgetfulness, leading me to awaken my return to practicing Critical Intent.

Interviewing and Evaluating

BEV works to enable one to have a keen sense of perceptually attuning in detecting an individual's manifesting specific attribute in the moment. As well, through this keen sense of focused imagery, we have been able to develop our ability to clearly detect targeted attributes manifesting in the person that we our evaluating.

The master focus of which I wrote about earlier, is the master key focus enabling us in getting to the heart of others quickly. When selecting a prospective candidate to work for your company, you need to consider using the master focus as a tool/technique when interviewing the candidate. Besides their technical skills, education, work experience and references for example, we need to consider the critical component/aspect of what we call one's EQ ability. Emotional quotient falls into the realm of one's focused intent in caring for others, amongst other related matters such as: one's emotional balance/stability, empathy towards others, getting along with others/teamwork etc. As I mentioned earlier, the master focused imagery overlaps with many EG qualities. With one foul swoop we can at once gain deep insight into one's EQ attributes. The critical component, however is the aspect of the potential employees Critical Intent measurement/valuation. Valuing and recognizing Critical Intent in another as being part of a critical component in hiring, will impact the company in a positive way, both in terms of it's profitability, and long- term success.

Evaluating your future partner

The same evaluation technique as BEV, can be used not only for evaluating/interviewing potential employees for hire, but also for example one's future partner/lover. Wouldn't you want to know something a little more than skin deep. Perhaps that person that takes an interest in you, is much better than you might think. For example, we are so deluded when it comes to falling for a person's appearance, that we may fall head over heels over the good looks and sexual component of an individual, thus making a foolish decision. Good physical looks in another is like having icing on the cake, so to speak. If we can find a partner with good physical looks and a good heart in the body of the cake, then that is a bonus for you. In an added manner, we could say that if your future partner is wealthy, has a good heart, and physically good looking, then again, its like you've hit a grand slam. However, there is a caveat to this, remember that the heart is the most important treasure that one can possess; don't stumble and fall over the material treasures and the treasures of the body- you might lose your way.

The depth and power of the focused intent in caring for the person before you, will not only reveal an expanded dimension of perception, but will also, by natural consequence bring forth the total picture into a clear focus, enabling you to make a wiser decision. Congratulations on seeing beauty in another, and congratulations on making a wise choice-you decide.

Security and Prevention

I used the practice of BEV when working as a Body Guard for a wealthy Chinese Businessman. At times prudence was the calling card that allowed for us to walk freely out of danger. The focused image of security became the mode at my disposal. Potentialities of outcomes exist in its latent state. Perceiving darkness and ill intent of others, becomes a red flag warning; to be evermore vigilant, and not allow a chain of events to lead you to a bad place. Always consider the reset button, walk away, rethink, and listen to your heart; there will be the light to lead you back to safety.

An owl is traditionally a symbol of wisdom, so we are neither doves nor hawks but owls, and we are vigilant when others are resting.

- URJIT PATEL

Benefits of Practicing Critical Intent

Practicing Critical Intent brings about a holistic improvement to the well being of our individualistic self. The domain of our chosen path, the decisions that we make along the way, both live to affect not only ourselves, but also others who cross our path. Since, we have internalized the tool of applying Critical Intent, then our path, therefore will be illuminated by the rays of our good heart. The elements of darkness and ignorance that surround and confront us at every moment, however, will be held at bay, as our focused intent of caring for others, provides us with the armored shield of our striking.

Amongst the many benefits of practicing Critical Intent, exist the following that is worth mentioning:

Intuition

Intuition is a vital sense that we posses, however, we fail to recognize its presence in our working life. The mental processing of our brain/mind function becomes separated from our intuition when we react passively to outside stimuli; in not being the master of our mind, we let our mind master us. To put it in another way, we have placed the cart before the horse in our movement forward. By, reacting, not from a well centered heart, but from a mind that is detached from our heart-the place where intuition resides, we find that our deluded mind, has no sense of insight into the subtle workings of life at any given moment. Whether you realize it or not, our mind can be said to be our worst enemy. Our mind can be easily manipulated, divorcing our senses from detecting and directing our life in the best way forward, based on the present moment.

The practice of Critical Intent, is a master component to our structure; an essential element tying in all necessary components to a solid operating structure. The components of health, financial, relationships, safety, support, goals, discipline, and our attitude, to name few, all become illuminated with the backing of practicing Critical Intent. As well, since our mind/brain become tuned and connected to our ongoing practice of Critical Intent, then we become the good captain of our ship, that moves forward in harmony with the fullness of life both within and without. And, our intuition, then, will naturally emerge from within, allowing the flow of such, to reach and signal, both our heart and mind to work within the spontaneous workings of life, moment to moment.

"Our bodies have five senses: touch, smell, taste, sight, hearing.

But not to be overlooked are the senses of our souls: intuition, peace,

foresight, trust, empathy. The differences between people lie in their use

of these senses; most people don't know anything about the inner senses

while a few people rely on them just as they rely on their physical senses,

and in fact probably even more."

-C. JOY BELL C.

"Intuition is seeing with the soul."
-DEAN KOONTZ

Communication

All of us are surrounded by some form of communication in our lives; serving as a thread that helps to integrate us in the operations in our life and the environment in which we live. We cannot in fact move forward in any meaningful and productive way without communications different aspects, roles, delivery, and consequences.

Beyond the normal communication lines such as, media news broadcasts-TV, radio, newspapers outlets, internet, books, gatherings, phones, and one to one live communication, there is as well, subtle lines of what we could call spin off lines of communication. Secondary lines, or vessels-like the analogy of collateral blood vessels, to the primary line of communication. For example, like the popular game called broken telephone line, where the first person on the line passes on a message to the person behind them in line, and the second person relates to the third person, and so on down the line, until the last person on the line has to repeat what was the original message; you can imagine why it is called broken telephone line. Such distortion from the original source of information, then becomes, twisted, incomplete and taken out of context. However, we in general are led to believe that these secondary lines are indeed, the truth. Furthermore, when we add in the human sinister ingredients of bias, partisan politics, greed, and half truths, then we have fallen fallacy to pseudo science. The engine oil of communication becomes dirty, and with it, so does the family of humanity. However, the practice of Critical Intent, the focused intent of caring for whomever crosses our path moment to moment, acts as an antidote, to the germ of misinformation, for without feeding the germ of bias, partisan politics, and greed, that stems from the human condition of ignorance, then misinformation does not have the fuel to burn and destroy the goodness of humanity.

On a personal level, our behavior, surrounding the workings of communication, is one to be taken seriously; for the consequences of our careless and reckless disregard for the workings of communication will come in time to bite your in your tail, hard, suddenly and unexpectedly, from where you may never recover. Practicing Critical Intent by itself, with disregard for common sense, does not guarantee your safety and protection from the cause and effect relationship with regards to communication. In fact, practicing Critical Intent, should make you more aware and diligent with respect to the strict workings that life plays, with regards to your behavior and mindfulness as it relates to your interplay with communication.

Are you aware, besides your self, of someone you know, or any group, business, Government etc. that have failed in good communication? Right, I thought so. So, what are you going to do about it? Are you learning from miscommunication, being a better communicator? What I'm about to say is hard based facts and consequences in not being a good communicator:

Take for example the recent Parkland, Florida shooting, where 17 student and faculty were killed by the perpetrator's gun shots, on, February 14, 2018. There is one outstanding error of communication worth noting that may have prevented this whole tragic event. According to media accounts, the shooter had posted on his social media account, his love of guns, and his desire to shoot up as many students as he could at the former high school from which he was expelled-not jut one message, but apparently other disturbing violent messages, indicating very clearly a potential threat to students. However, shockingly, these posts were never acted upon. Uh-we say? Everyone has a responsibility either knowingly or unknowingly, to safeguard our community from any perceived form of potential threat. I say, unknowingly, because we must not be complacent in our indifference to others, but rather, to always be in the present mindset of using our senses-eyes, ears, and so on, to consider, as in the practice of Critical Intent, the well being of our fellow brethren.

Never assume anything as being looked after; refer to Murphy's laws:

1) "In any field of endeavor, anything that can go wrong, will go wrong"
2) "Left to themselves, things always go from bad to worse."
3) "If there is a possibility of several things going wrong, the one that will go wrong, is the one that will cause the most damage."
4) "Nature always sides with the hidden flaw."
5) "If everything seems to be going well, you have obviously overlooked something."

-Wikipedia

The art of communication is the language of leadership.

- JAMES HUMES

The single biggest problem in communication is the

illusion that it has taken place.

- GEORGE BERNARD SHAW

Social media websites are no longer performing an envisaged function of creating a positive communication link among friends, family and professionals. It is a veritable battleground, where insults fly from the human quiver, damaging lives, destroying self-esteem and a person's sense of self-worth.

- ANTHONY CARMONA

The Great Unity of Brother and Sisterhood in our drive towards Happiness and Peace

Critical Intent helps to unite us, the environment, and our place within the universe. Our inherent capacity, that unites us all, is our quest, working for happiness and peace for all. Despite the divisions, that seemingly separate humanity around the globe, from a deeper and higher perceptive regarding the fundamental workings of life itself, we must stop to consider, the grand scheme of life and the universe.

The fundamental creative force and function of the universe is compassion. All who unite behind this fundamental nature of compassion, will merge into a sense of oneness with life and the universe.

Practicing Critical Intent forces and trains our default tendency to move beyond the petty reactive mode that consumes are every moment, in relationship to our encounter with those whom we dislike. We sabotage and derail, our very self, when we allow our ego/lower self, to dictate our feelings and thoughts in an unenlightened vicious circle of unnecessary suffering, discontent, anger and depression to only name a few, to continue unabated, when we react with such negatively to those who stimulate such feelings within us. Reset, now, at this moment to consider what it is that we are working towards as a human race, and our relationship to all that there is, was, and will be on into eternity. Do not allow such short sightedness, to stop your continuous movement forward towards this one common goal that we all share as humanity- the happiness and peace of all humankind.

Critical Intent can serve as a valuable exercise to merge our life to that basic driving force that pulsates throughout life. Not caring to even consider some sort of focused intent to engage our compassionate heart to that of another who crosses our path, is a deluded state of fundamental ignorance, an unenlightened manifestation of our lesser self. Part of the problem, with this whole matter, is that we do not know any better; we have never been taught otherwise. Who is to blame for this unbelievable mis-discovery, that we have failed to recognize- that my friend, takes me by surprise as well!

Are you willing to take a look at this misgiving, reflect, and have the courage to consider the basis of the reasoning and logic, as to why the focused intent of caring for the person in front of you, matters not only for your own advancement and growth, but also for the person in front of you, your family, and by extension and ripple effect, society, the world, and on into past, present, and future generations of your linkage/connection.

"The world is round so that friendship may encircle it."

- PIERRE TEILHARD DE CHARDIN

Reflecting the Moon

How beautiful that we experience the moons reflection amongst the waters of earth. For thousands of years we have bonded our souls to the night sky that never sleeps. Let me give you an analogy to the moon and its' casting reflection upon the clear waters that surround us.

Let's say that the moon in the night sky represents all that is good in life and the universe. The casting of the moon's beneficial powers to humankind, can, let's say act as a metaphor. And further, let's say that the water below reflects the beauty of the moon upon its waters. Let's say that we are the water, and our water can be clear, muddy, or anything in between. We strive to reflect the casting moon's light to its fullest, however, we need to consider the clarity of our own water.

How then, can we make our water clear? The beauty aspect, of which I wrote about earlier, is a key component to the making of clear water in our life. All darkness or muddied water in our life is the antithesis to the shining ray of beauty or clear water that we attempt to emulate. Our task, therefore, is to purify our water, so that beauty and fortune can be reflected in all aspects of our life. Note, however, that all darkness or impurities in our life are inherent and part of the human condition. We can never eliminate or flush out the nature of darkness in our life, but we can at least, live each moment in the beauty that we inherently possess. The darkness is always there as an inherent potential, but the light, clarity and beauty can be operational and in control of our life moment to moment, if we so choose to do so.

Cleaning Process

- Close examination of self.
- Seeking out others feedback, regarding our behavior
- Realize that striving to become like clear water is beneficial to our life.
- Being mindful of our thoughts, and how we react to life, moment to moment.
- Write up to 100 good things about yourself-small, medium, or large successes.
- Write up 100 vices

Potential barriers to cleaning:

- Perfectionism
- Shame, guilt
- Pride
- Laziness
- Denial
- Examining all 11 attributes/categories that I wrote about in the section titled perception/BEV

"Don't tell me the moon is shining; show me

the glint of light on broken glass."

- ANTON CHEKHOV

"Everyone is a moon, and has a dark side which
he never shows to anybody."

- MARK TWAIN

"The moon is a loyal companion.
It never leaves. It's always there, watching, steadfast, knowing us in our
light and dark moments, changing forever just as we do. Every day it's a
different version of itself. Sometimes weak and wan, sometimes strong
and full of light. The moon understands what it means to be human.
Uncertain. Alone. Cratered by imperfections."

- TAHEREH MAFI, Shatter Me

"Yours is the light by which my spirit's born:
- you are my sun, my moon, and all my stars."

- E.E. CUMMINGS

"We are all like the bright moon, we still have our darker side."

- KAHLIL GIBRAN

Soul Cleaning

Our daily life will always face opportunities of challenge. One of the biggest challenges to our life is in keeping the integrity of our soul. Beauty or clear water, can both act as manifestations of our soul. In drawing an analogy to our soul, you could compare our soul to the structure of a big building. In maintaining the integrity of a building's structure, constant upkeep and maintenance is required. Likewise, our soul too requires constant upkeep in maintaining its beauty and purity.

Every day we are presented with choices; decisions that will impact upon our soul. Ask yourself, "does this decision align with my soul?" Listening to your heart will help guide you in the right direction, and thus keep the pure alignment of your heart and soul in place. Besides listening to your heart there are some other key aspects that are critical to protecting your soul.

Courage

Be the lion that you are. Cowardice, is not the making of a lion. When being confronted with your fears, doubt, and timidity for example, we can enfold ourselves in the image of a lion. Life applauds those who have the courage to stand up and not give in to the easy route of passivity and retreat. However daunting of intimidating whatever it is that we face, keep in mind that having courage will add beauty and character to yourself.

Hope/faith/prayer/confidence

In a collective grouping of these four elements, we find that the way forward in our life depends upon these four elements to encase our soul in the rock of that which is good. Hope is the everlasting virtue of survival, in these times in which we live. Never lose hope amongst the wasteland of darkness and negativity that prevail in our society today. Faith in the unseen is the virtue of our connection to all that there is. The unseen virtue of our faith is also our expectation and humble union with life itself.

Prayer is an active immersion of our life to the greatness and beauty within and without life's existence, and confidence is the striking hammer, that sounds the bell of all the other three former elements.

"Success is not final, failure is not fatal:

it is the courage to continue that counts."

- WINSTON S. CHURCHILL

Optimism is the faith that leads to achievement.

Nothing can be done without hope and confidence

-HELEN KELLER

Prayer is the key of the morning and the bolt of the evening.

-MAHATMA GANDHI

Challenge

A fine steel sword is forged through a repeated tempering and smelting process, producing an extremely strong work of art. We too, need to be like a strong steel sword, being able to endure and withstand the trials and tribulations of life. Youth especially need to be mindful of the importance of challenging themselves throughout their youth. Building a strong character in one's youth will aid one in protecting the purity of their soul, where one proudly walks through life with a strong forbearance facing life's vicissitudes.

The Ultimate Measure of a man is not where he stands in

moments of comfort and convenience, but where

he stands at times of challenge and controversy.

- MARTIN LUTHER KING, JR.

Seeking Truth/Openness

"The truth shall set you free;" that phrase rings the bell to our awakening of now in this moment of truth. Do we really seek the truth? Resisting the truth, becomes the darkness over our soul. The light of truth, and the light of openly seeking the truth, allows the blossoming of our soul to be the center piece of our life. Life is strict, and it is up to us to choose the path of our seeking.

Beauty is truth's smile when she beholds her

own face in a perfect mirror.

- RABINDRANATH TAGORE

Polishing

Polishing a diamond can act as a good metaphor for our life. A polished diamond shines forth its inherent beauty; just like the beauty of our soul that can also shine when polished. What does it mean to polish our soul?

Polishing of our soul requires daily conscious effort on our part. When we greet the morning, what is the first thing that we do when we awake? Besides being refreshed from our sleep, our soul too has been at our side of rest. Get down on your knees and polish the dirt on the floor of your soul- metaphorically speaking. Every day we need to polish, dust off any dirt that has accumulated in our life. A constant polishing will keep the beauty of our soul to shine. And the daily practice of polishing our life returns us to the essence of all that is good. Whatever is your religion, philosophy or spiritual practice, consider this as your place of rejuvenation, renewal, and reviving. Your prayer and practice that unites and brings you into a good place is your act of polishing. Ask yourself how you feel after your act of polishing. Polishing your life includes, self reflection, apology and determination to make good, reaching out and sharing with others. We are not alone, and as such, we need to practice polishing for both self and others.

The soul is placed in the body like a rough diamond, and must

be polished, or the luster of it will never appear.

- DANIEL DEFOE

Innocence is like polished armor; it adorns and defends.

- ROBERT SOUTH

What we were never taught

 Key principles about living our life now, are becoming part of our everyday living. Principles that are taken for granted and obvious to us now, were however, not so, in our not so distant past. Why, in all the years of our schooling and parenting were we not taught about such important principles as, for example, not holding onto resentment, the importance of respecting others, as having an impact on both our own life and that of others, polishing our life from the inside, so that we can illuminate our beauty from the inside, the importance of our behavior, as being crucial for both our own life, and affecting others and the world at large, the inter-dependence that we all share in common with others, and what my book is about, the critical importance of having the focused intent of caring for the person who crosses our path moment to moment. Whatever the speculation of such, we are here now to teach our youth the lessons of life that we have come to know. Todays youth are our future, and as such, it is up to us adults now, to impart upon them, our valuable lessons of life that we have gained through our own life experiences. Just imagine, the life of so many youth, changing and impacting the world, to move into a better place, than the world has ever known.

Youth is the gift of nature, but age is a work of art.

- STANISLAW JERZY LEC

PART SIX

SUSTAINING CRITICAL INTENT

Passion is the genesis of genius

-TONY ROBBINS

ONCE YOU HAVE grasped and determined to live with Critical Intent, you are ready to venture out to a new and exciting world that awaits you. How you come to embrace living with Critical Intent is your undertaking of a reflective introspection of your own life, of your own value system. You are a magnificent being who can walk the path of higher plains. I'm not asking you to give up anything in your life; you just need to add a critical component of having the focused intent of caring for others' well-being moment to moment in your daily life. I invite you to join me in a new- found path of emancipation from the darkened restraining path that has railroaded you toward a conclusive end of inevitable regret at your final resting place. You have a choice, a new direction to take you forward, to liberate you into a new dimension of all-embracing love for self and others who surround you. Take the choice that is before you; the time is right for such an undertaking. Demonstrate to yourself, others, and the universe that you're here, now, to awaken to what is yours to claim. I claim the life and brightness that I have always held but have failed to awaken.

Sustaining the flow of Critical Intent continuously day to day cannot be taken for granted. Life is a constant battle of triumph and victory over the dark, devilish aspects of life. The force and power that impede our entry into the light of goodness do not sleep. We should not sleep, either. Ours is a constant battle with the inherent dark side of our life. We have the tools and capacity to win over the dark forces that shut us down. You have your religion, whatever it is, your practice of faith and discipline, whatever it is, to give you the strength, wisdom, and power to surmount your obstacles and challenges in daily life. Use what you have; practice to the limits of your capacity. Do not slacken in your efforts, for today, in this time of our life, you face unprecedented challenges that did not exist before to the degree that they exist now. Embrace the challenge of insidious workings that are all so pervasive in societies today. Those challenges are the masks of greed, stupidity, anger, disunity, chaos, and neglect to our fellow brethren, to name a few, that run rampant under the guise of a passive comfort. They are destroying our will to fight back and reclaim the great beings that we are.

  Be mindful of the reality facing you every day; determine to fight your weakness every day, and as long as you practice and take action in the realm of having the focused intent in caring for others, then you will become stronger, lighter, and more brilliant each day. Do not be discouraged at your failings; learn form such; arise and try again. Your courageous efforts are not alone; you are leading an unseen multitude of brethren who are waiting for your victory, who are following you from the unseen, who upon your victory will emerge together with you in glorious celebration. Your individual efforts are the key to the start of reversal in the direction that we are all heading. Be proud of your achievements, share with others, write the script of your destiny so that we all can be in the company of those who share the movement toward a better place.

Concentrate all your thoughts upon the work at hand.

The sun's rays do not burn until brought to a focus.

-ALEXANDER GRAHAM BELL

You don't have to be great to start,

but you have to start to be great.

-ZIG ZIGLAR

EXERCISE TO READY AND STRENGTHEN
CRITICAL INTENT

PRACTICING GRATITUDE

WHEN YOU CAN feel gratitude permeating your being wherever you may walk, then the oneness of your connection to yourself and all of life becomes an opening for your life. Open yourself up and ride the wave of an expanded heart. Be the person who shines with appreciation and positive light.

One exercise that works to engage you to a place of peace within yourself is the practice of writing down something for which you are grateful. I started from day one to write down, or in my case text, into my Android phone one thing that I was grateful for that day. The reason that I texted into my phone was to send it to my co-worker. On day two, or simply the next day, I then texted two things that I was grateful for that day, and so on right until day thirty, when I texted thirty things that I was grateful for.

You will find that at the end of thirty days, your perspective about life will have changed. You will not be the same person and yet, of course, you are the same person. Be that person who you really are. You are not an ungrateful person. You are not meant to live out your life in meanness and negative complaining.

Put yourself out to the spectrum of what lies before you. Continue to have the mindset of noting that for which you are grateful. Look around you; see all that is provided for you, good and bad. Yes, even the bad is an opportunity that awaits your awakening to such. Give thanks to everything that is presented before you. Be the transformer, be the master, be the painter who pours the liquid of your unique alchemy to the canvas of life the surrounds you.

Being grateful opens your life to others, bringing you one step closer in being the person who has the motivation and desire to practice **Critical Intent.**

Mindfulness

As studies indicate, being mindful stimulates portions of the brain activity to light up and can be measured scientifically. Being mindful, as an exercise, helps us to stay on track in our focused intent in caring for the person(s) before us moment to moment. When you first wake up in the morning, greet the day with anticipated goodness, adventure, and the continued practice of Critical Intent. The morning is the gold of our start for the rest of the day; the cause to set our day on a continuous track of freshness, energy and determination, casting you into the beckoning waters, sailing you through, come what may. The continual mindfulness exercise in the morning of giving thought to your determination to continuously be in the mode of Critical Intent is a good start to begin your day.

Reflection

On the other end of our time spectrum awaits night time; a time of reflection. Ask yourself, "how was my day today?" What mistakes did I make today? Reflecting on how you reacted and dealt with different situations during the day, will often lead you to an awareness of seeing things in a different perspective, for example, you might ask yourself: "would I act differently if again given the same situation?" Reflection acts to reinforce change in our life, to shake and awake up the spontaneous genius in your life, that allows you to act with wisdom and confidence in every situation.

The real man smiles in trouble, gathers strength from distress,

and grows brave by reflection.

-THOMAS PAINE

Surrendering

Do not try to control everything. Relax and allow the unfolding of what is; embrace and accept the present situation in a manner of allowance, patience, understanding and wisdom. Nothing occurs by accident, and you are not the maker and director of things that are out of your control. Take my point as a consideration to contend with, in your tendency to control everything that is taking place. What I'm saying is not absolute, and it is up to your intuition and wisdom to decide what is the best course of action to take in any given situation. But if you always take the stance of controlling every situation, then you will have failed in the department of surrender. Surrendering to allow the situation to unfold, does not mean that you are being weak and passive; what surrendering means, is that you are attentive to the firing up of your fine senses of listening, seeing, and feeling, to name a few. So as an exercise, I suggest, try breaking your stubborn ego aside, and listen to the natural unfolding sounding of life's pulse, like the ebb and flow of the crashing waves. At times ride the cresting wave, and at other times sink with the flow.

"Surrender to what is.

Let go of what was.

Have faith in what will be."

-SONIA RICOTTI

Stepping outside of your comfort zone

Be the one that ventures out into the unknown, that mystic darkness and light, both beckoning your venture into possibilities yet to come. By challenging and actively moving into arenas of the unknown, the doors of opportunity, growth, and positive change await. So, why stop and frame ourselves within the parameters of the known, when outside those known parameters lies the potential arena to accentuate, open, and broaden our unmasking of the great potential that is waiting to be unleashed to its full potential from within us? Consider then, what it takes for you to make the mark in both your life and that of others. The growth and expansion of your outlay into other fields of endeavor, will in turn touch others, and they in turn will touch others-ripple effect. So, as an exercise to consider, I would suggest allowing yourself, from time to time, to contemplate, meditate and pray, on becoming a person of courage to fear not the unknown, but to believe in yourself with confidence, that I will do whatever it takes to be a person from which others will benefit, not only now, but into the eternal future.

The best things in life are often waiting for you at the

exit ramp of your comfort zone.
-KAREN SALMANSOHN

The comfort zone is the great enemy to creativity;

moving beyond it necessitates intuition, which in turn

configures new perspectives and conquers fears.
-DAN STEVENS

The Death of Charlie

In memory of our beloved dog, Charlie, the one who started my journey of Critical Intent; we who hear back to those unforgettable moments that passed between us, I owe it to him, in honor of his life spent amongst our midst, to pay tribute to such a worthy and significant life that he played in the contribution and development of Critical Intent.

Charlie lived out his life, unaware, of his valuable contribution to humanity, through my dog experience. The many hours and days of walks that transpired between us and the many neighbors and community fellows that witnessed the behavior of his nick name, "Run away Charlie," will remain with us forever. For Charlie, always had to be kept on a leash, otherwise he would just take off. During his almost fourteen years life with us, seven times he ran off from our hold, and each time we thought, "that was it," but incredibly, we were always able to retrieve him. Charlie had no sense of oncoming cars, would run anywhere a scent took him, and would just keep on going, even if we yelled at him to stop. There was a mission to be seen and realized for this dog named Charlie. The time had come on December 07, 2016, to lay Charlie to rest, in his composure of a mission completed.

Death is not the greatest loss in life.

The greatest loss is what dies inside us while we live.

-NORMAN COUSINS

LIFE SPACE

As life would have it, there is one last critical essential teaching that I would like to share with you. All practices of "Critical Intent," the focused intent in caring for others, and the training and practicing of "Bull's-eye Vision," serve as prerequisites to the final and most important practice that you can engage in, and that is to, **"OPEN UP YOUR LIFE."**

To begin, our lives are very much closed regardless of our good intentions. It takes the following, critical component ingredient, to complete the recipe/formula in opening of your life. For starters, just recognizing that there is such a thing as being closed vs being open and recognizing some of the following traits as being impediments to our opening:

- Negative anger
- Irritation
- Anxiety/worry
- Self-centeredness
- Being judgemental
- Lacking joy
- Being narrow minded
- Showing vanity
- Not caring for others
- Engaging in gossip
- Nonsense talk
- Being dishonest

- Insincerity
- Not seeking to learn and grow
- Self-righteousness
- Being critical of others and quick to find fault
- Jealously

You get the picture

How to Become an Open Person

1) The first technique that I used at the beginning and found to be very helpful in allowing me to loosen the grip of a closed life, was to say the following to myself when anything came my way that could cause me irritation or anger. For example, if a car were to cut me off, or I would be stuck in traffic while driving, I would say to myself,

"It doesn't matter," "It doesn't, matter," # "It doesn't matter."

2) **Appreciation**

Have gratitude for everything-even the bad things that come your way, for example, appreciate the beauty of life, nature, family, and everything that you have. As well appreciate difficult times and challenges, for they will strengthen and forge a strong character.

3) Apply the focused intent in observing another's closeness/openness. You will clearly see the blockers to the opening of their life, ie: the list of ingredients that I listed for a closed life. Vow to yourself, to never be like that. Have empathy and understanding of others self -imposed imprisonment to their openness.

4) Have the courage and boldness to point out to your friends and acquaintances what you can see as impediments to their life's opening. Share with others your experience in freeing up, away from the impediments that kept you being closed. Just share, and not judge others. Be calm and genuinely helpful in your advice to others.

5) Whatever is your religion, philosophy or spiritual practice, use your faith and practice to help enable you to open your life-to all that is. Open beyond a self-centered self, to connect with what is great. Plug into the vastness of life and creation of the universe-whatever it is that you want to call it. Without some spiritual discipline practice of some sort, then it becomes extremely difficult to open your self on your own. We need a mentor, guide, teacher, discipline and practice that we can lay as a foundation to our life.

CONCLUSION

TIME TO REVIEW YOU PLACE OF REFERENCE
TO THE OPENING LINES OF THIS BOOK

Well, what do you think?

Do you feel that you have shaped any of the following qualities listed below?

Peace within yourself

Gratitude alone will give you a measure of peace.

Harmony in your relationships

One can lead the joyous dance of life out of darkness and into the harmony of a caring heart.

Living with confidence, wisdom, and courage

Strike the fire of your newfound vision; a focused vision that directs you from the inwardness of your heart towards the hearts of others.

Confidence and wisdom operate together when your place of reference lies deep within the connection of your heart to the compassionate pulse of life itself.

Courage of your life, springs to life when you awaken to your mission and purpose to create value both for yourself and others.

Being an outstanding light to others

Be the light that you are; be the guide that guides your light into the darkness of people's hearts, and you will be the light.

Living to your full potential

Bursting forth from your smaller self onto the canvas of an expanded life, you have awakened the lion in your life. Be that lion that roars to the awakening and trembling of the uniqueness and power of your life, unleashed by the focus of your newfound intent.

Being a leader to others

Others are waiting for your entry into the fray of their troubled life. Your uniqueness is your key to unlocking the movement toward helping others in their own quest of their uniqueness to lead a life of value and purpose. One person being encouraged by the touch of your life qualifies you as being a leader. Judge not others as being the same as you and vice versa; others are not your comparison to the input of value that you alone possess upon your entry into the lives of others. Hold your head high; emit the confidence, courage, and wisdom that you now bring to others. Your leadership and guidance will plant the seeds of eventual blossoming in others.

Living an abundant life

Gratitude is abundance. Living in this moment now contains the abundance of your life now. Tomorrow has not yet arrived, but now in this moment, you can live to your fullest. Display your focused intent in caring for the person in front of you, and you will create abundance for your life. Build upon your effort, accelerate your growth, and you will acquire abundance. What is it that your life needs now? As you become more and more the superhero that I spoke of before, the magnetism and virtue of your life will gain abundance. Your needs, one by one, will become fulfilled, for you are bathing in the light of abundance. Strengthen your faith day by day. Live so that others may rejoice now, and in the future, for your continued efforts in making a difference to someone out there, will explode forth a rippling effect, causing you, society, and the world to move into a better place.

Critical Intent exists in the light of something that is there for your taking. What you do with your life is up to you; your lessons and experiences are your uniqueness, your walk amongst us in sharing with all of us a commonality of humanity's striving for a better world, now and in the future.

Your practicing of Critical Intent is an avenue that will lead you into a new direction that only you suffice to name it-your journey. We are not alone amongst the personage of humankind, and your life is shared by all of us. The world will change, you will change, and all that you know will change. However, all that there is to change, is up to you now. Do not think that your presence is an unaccountable mark of contribution into the mix of our ongoing struggle to make for a better world. Take the tool of Critical Intent that I have offered. Mine is only a voice of many, who partake to share to others, that walk the same path in a shared struggle of humanity's quest in arising to the glory and magnificence of what it means to be human. Use your talents of your inherent blessings, share with others your struggles, learning and experience, for there are many who are seeking to join with you and others their quest for a better life and a better world. Be that one, of such an individual, who makes a profound difference and transformation for self, others and the world at large. Critical Intent offers you a way forward into the chaos and indifference that surrounds us all at this moment. The continuance of your sanity is at test, now in these times. Take up your mantle of ignited fury, slay the dark beast of ignorance, and march into the fray of a deliverable path of clearing, that will be the light of your enduring record.

Life space

And finally, have the vision to open your life at every moment. Your constant struggle to keep your life open and expanding every moment will be your constant challenge. Our default position of a closed life takes time to adjust; constant practice and mindfulness on this point is essential if we ever want to break our cycle, and shift our pendulum away from a closed, dark and deluded life, to a life of being fully opened, expanding daily to the depths of life itself.

SERVICES

Individual one on one:

-can meet in person, or face zoom/skype; telephone and e-mail also available

-Offer workshops, seminars, retreats, office presentations and private functions.

Please feel free to contact me at my email: 33jmhunter@gmail.com

to book an appointment or any inquires that you may have.

Thanks,

John Hunter